Eucharistic Hymns

From

The Catholic Hymnal

Ellen Doll Jones & Noel Jones, Editors

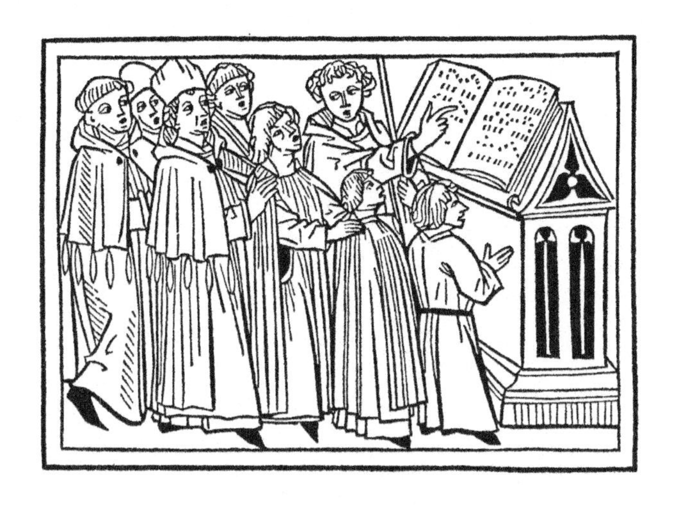

WWW.THECATHOLICHYMNAL.COM

According To Thy Gracious word
And I Shall See His Face
Be Known To Us In Breaking Bread
Deck Thyself, My Soul, With Gladness
Draw Nigh And Take The Body Of The Lord
Drop, Drop, Slow Tears
Hail! Thou Living Bread
Here, O My Lord, I See Thee Face To Face
Holy! Holy! Holy! Holy!
In This Sacrament, Sweet Jesus
Jesus, Food Of Angels
Jesus, Gentlest Savior
Jesus, Jesus, Come To Me
Jesus, Lord, Be Thou My Own
Jesus, My Lord, My God, My All
Jesus, Thou Art Coming
My God, And Is Thy Table Spread
My God, Thy Table Now Is Spread
Now, My Tongue, The Mystery
O Bread Of Heav n
O Christ, To You We Bring Our Weary Souls
O Food That Weary Pilgrims Love
O Food, The Pilgrim Needeth
O God, Unseen, Yet Ever Near
O Godhead Hid
O Jesus Christ, Redeemer
O Jesus, Thou The Glory Art
O Jesus, Lord, Most Mighty king
O Jesus, Lord, Remember
O Lord, I Am Not Worthy
O Sacrament Most Holy
Panis Angelicus
Peace, Perfect Peace
Soul Of My Savior
Sweet Sacrament Divine!
The King Of Heav n His Table Spreads
The Very Angels Bread
This Is The Hour Of Banquet And Of Song
We Thee adore
What Happiness Can Equal Mine?
Word Of God To Earth Descending

THE CATHOLIC HYMNAL™
Under Development

PUBLISHED

Eucharistic Hymns
Hymnbook
CD

Hymns To Mary
Hymnbook
CD

An Anthology of Hymns from The Catholic Hymnal
Eucharistic Hymns
Benediction Hymns
Hymns To Mary

Blank pages included to eliminate
page turns by organists and singers.

www.thecatholichymnal.com

©2009 Frog Music Press
www.frogmusic.com

The Catholic Hymnal
201 CR 432, Englewood, TN 37329

423 887-7594

Gregorian Chant formed the first hymns. Chant has two forms, syllabic and melismatic. Some of the earliest hymns are chants, set to a repeating, mainly syllabic text, with a bit of melisma thrown in. Examples include Adoro Te Devote.

As the use of local language for devotions outside of Mass became popular, writers, composers and eventually publishers rose to the challenge. English hymns were commonly published as text only, no music, in the mid to late 1800's. By the early 1900's, published hymn books which combined text and music were popular. By studying these old hymn books, one can trace the development as hymns as we know them today - from single line chant; to chant melodies harmonized in block harmony; and finally, four vocal parts written on two staves.

Early 1800's hymns were written with the basic note being a half note. In the early 1900's, this changed and the quarter note the most common note length, though the eighth note was also popular.

How can you use these hymns? We will, upon receipt of your email, permit copying of hymns you request. Or you may wish to order hymnals for your choir. But we also offer you the ability to purchase and download a digital PDF file of this book, which will give you license to reproduce hymns to create bulletins and song books.

We enjoy hearing from people who sing from our music, so please drop us a note.

Noel Jones, AAGO
noeljones@usit.net

According to Thy Gracious Word

TALLIS' ORDINAL 86. 86. THOMAS TALLIS
JAMES MONTGOMERY

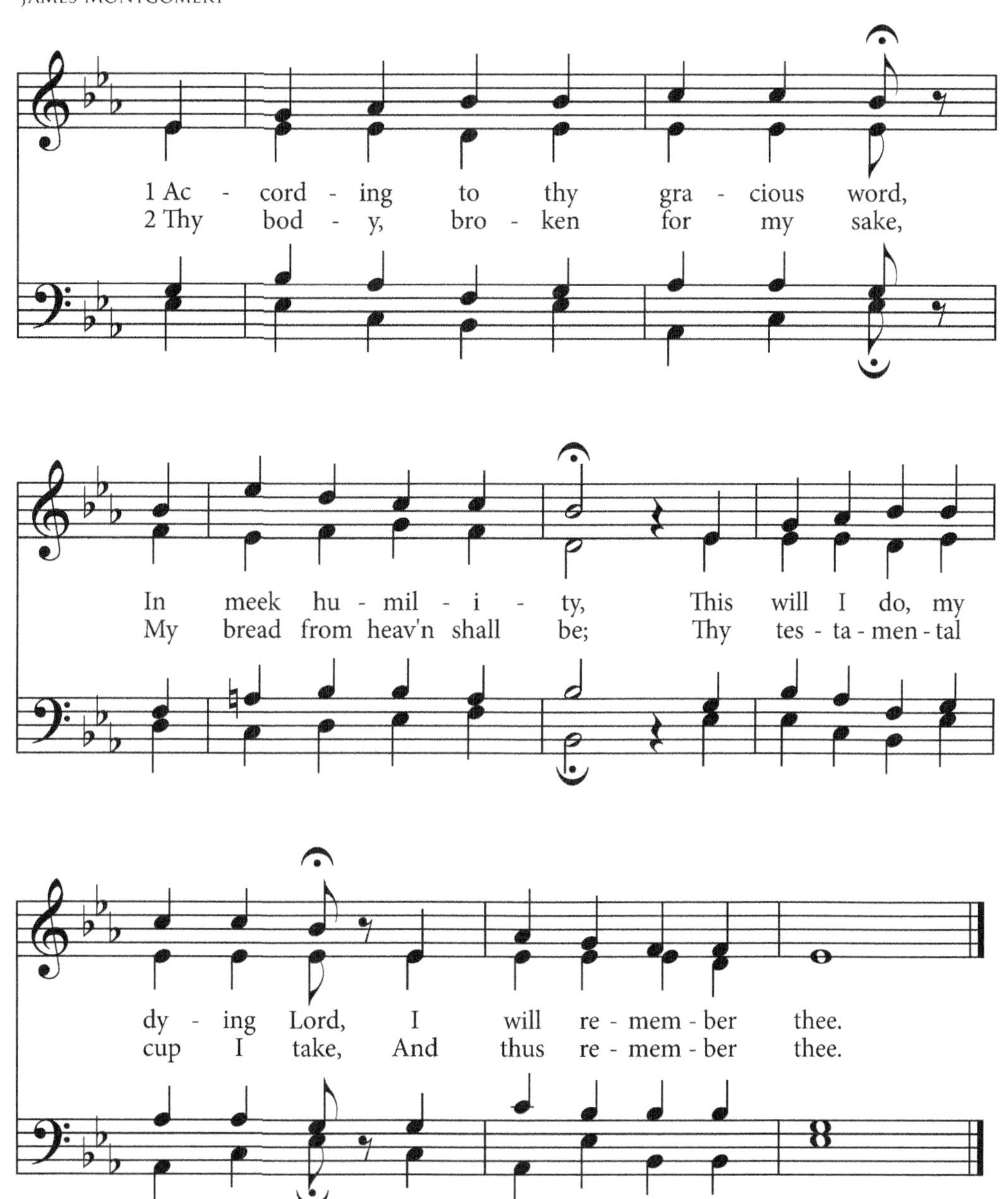

1 According to thy gracious word, In meek humility, This will I do, my dying Lord, I will remember thee.

2 Thy body, broken for my sake, My bread from heav'n shall be; Thy testamental cup I take, And thus remember thee.

AND I SHALL SEE HIS FACE

OLIVE 8.6.8.6 NOEL JONES
WILLIAM COWPER

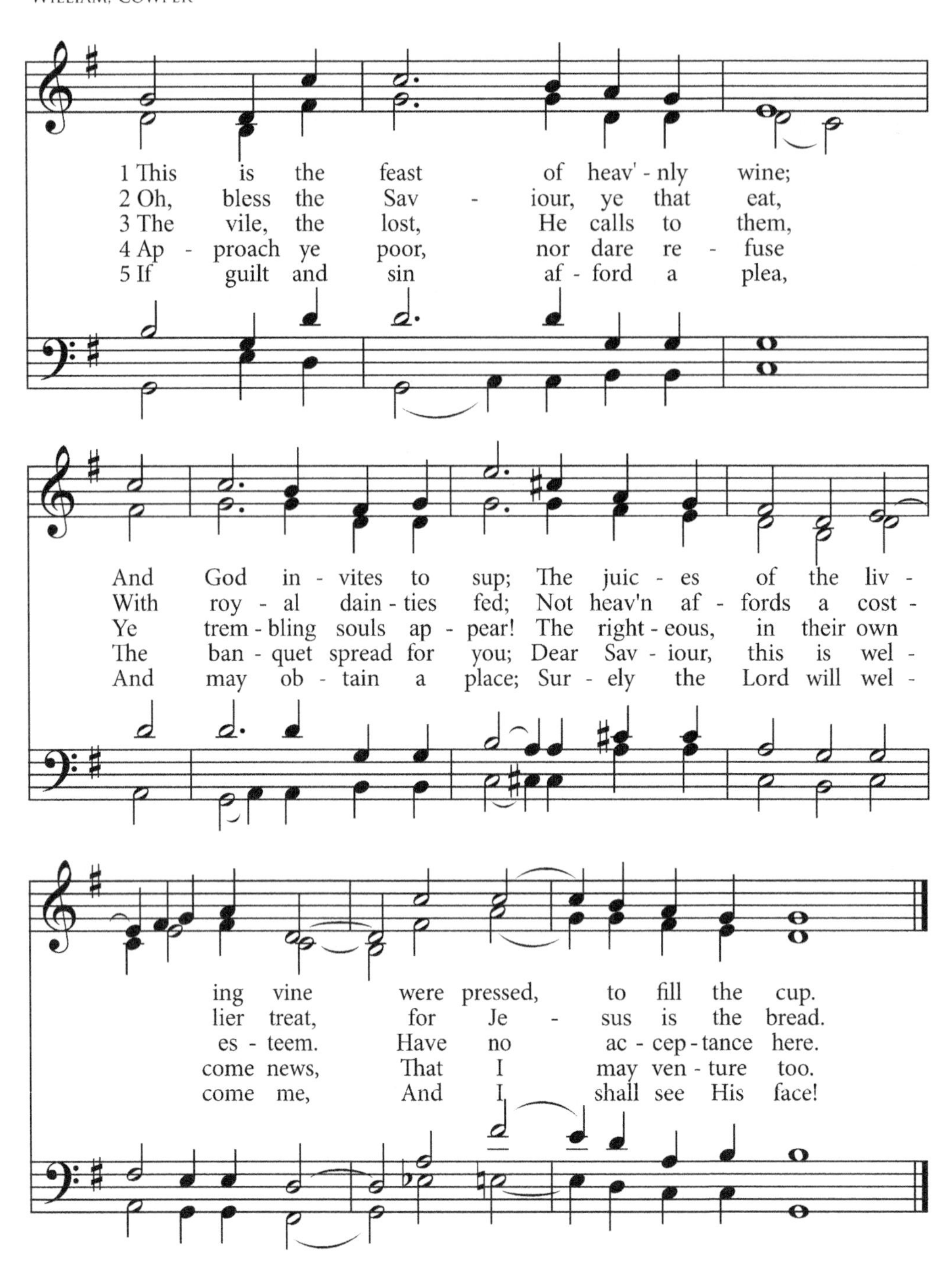

1 This is the feast of heav'nly wine; And God invites to sup; The juices of the living vine were pressed, to fill the cup.
2 Oh, bless the Saviour, ye that eat, With royal dainties fed; Not heav'n affords a costlier treat, for Jesus is the bread.
3 The vile, the lost, He calls to them, Ye trembling souls appear! The righteous, in their own esteem. Have no acceptance here.
4 Approach ye poor, nor dare refuse The banquet spread for you; Dear Saviour, this is welcome news, That I may venture too.
5 If guilt and sin afford a plea, And may obtain a place; Surely the Lord will welcome me, And I shall see His face!

BE KNOWN TO US IN BREAKING BREAD

SONG SIXTY-SEVEN 86. 86 ORLANDO GIBBONS
JAMES MONTGOMERY

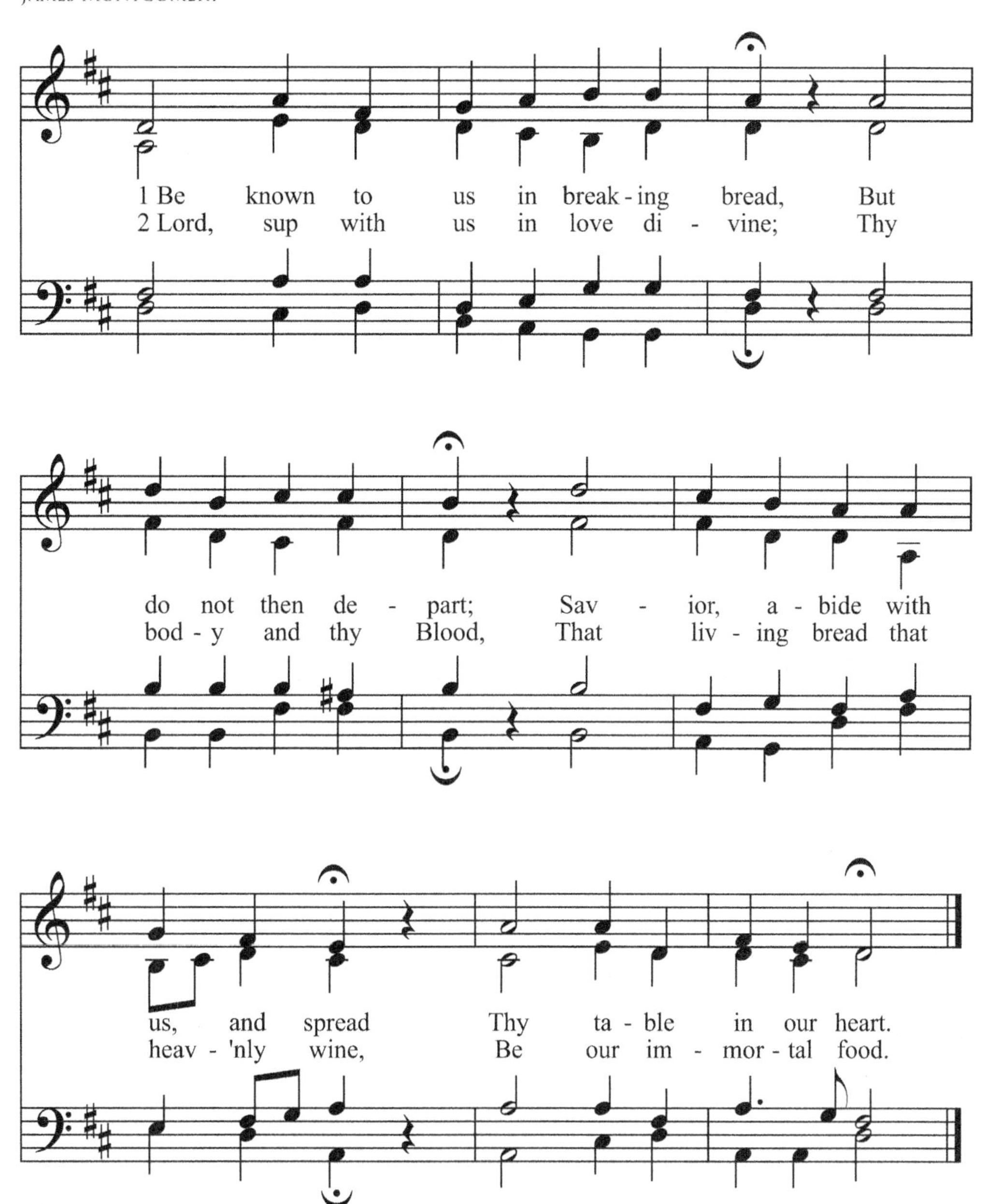

1. Be known to us in breaking bread, But do not then depart; Savior, abide with us, and spread Thy table in our heart.
2. Lord, sup with us in love divine; Thy body and thy Blood, That living bread that heav'nly wine, Be our immortal food.

BE KNOWN TO US IN BREAKING BREAD

ST. FLAVIAN 86. 86
JAMES MONTGOMERY

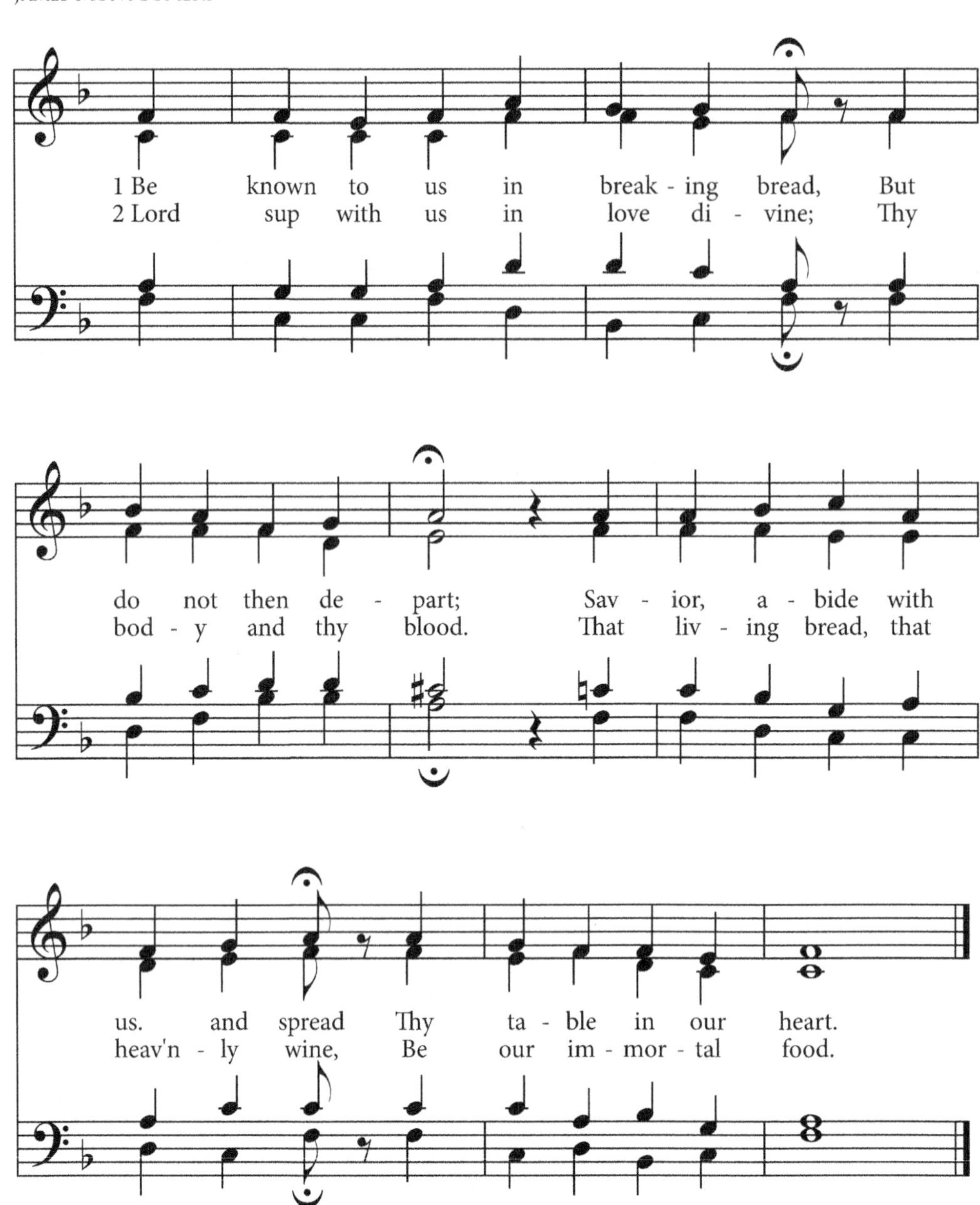

1 Be known to us in breaking bread, But do not then depart; Savior, abide with us. and spread Thy table in our heart.

2 Lord sup with us in love divine; Thy body and thy blood. That living bread, that heav'nly wine, Be our immortal food.

DECK THYSELF, MY SOUL, WITH GLADNESS

SCHMUEKE DICH - 88. 88. 88. 88. JOHANN CRUEGER
JOHANN FRANCK

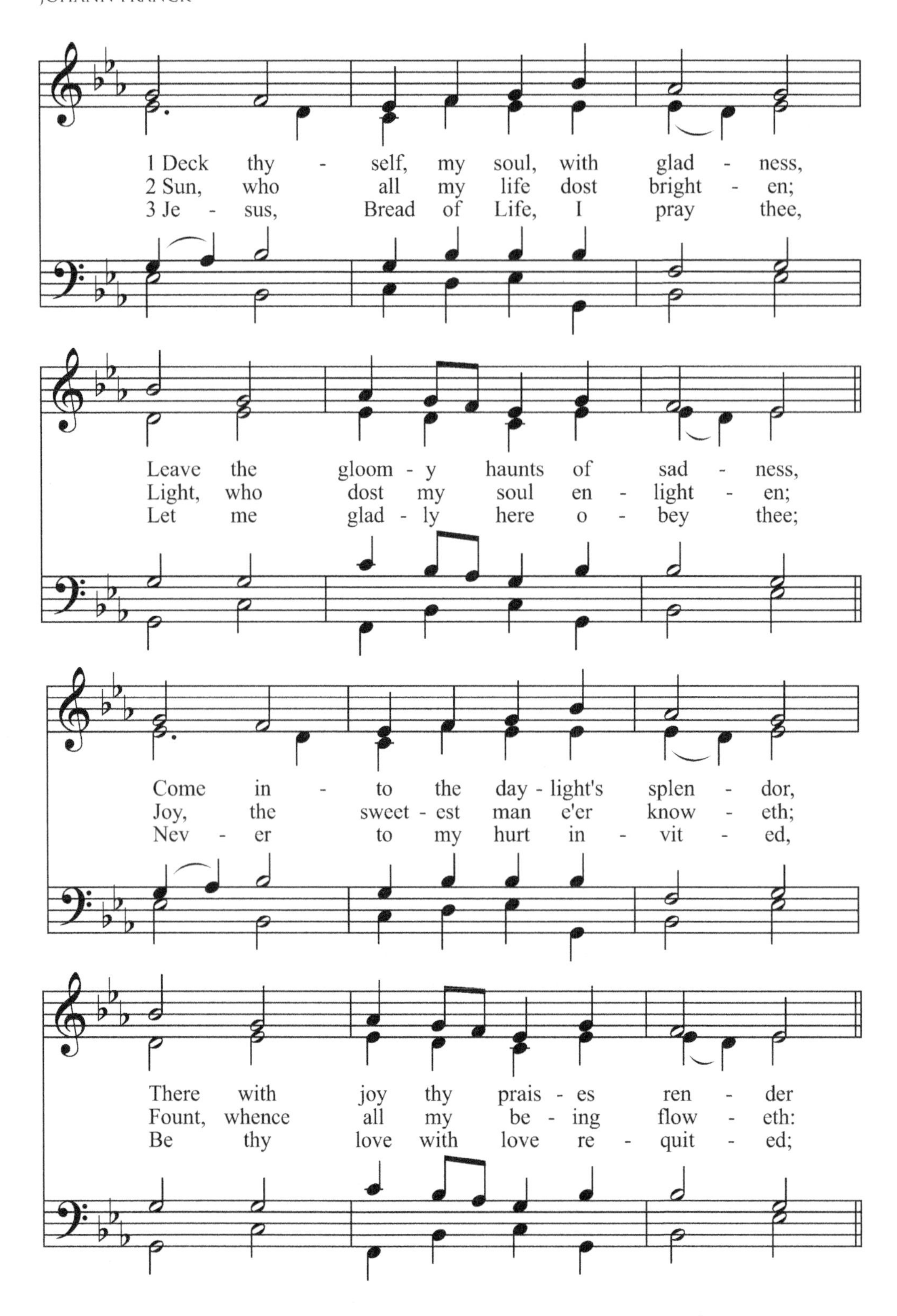

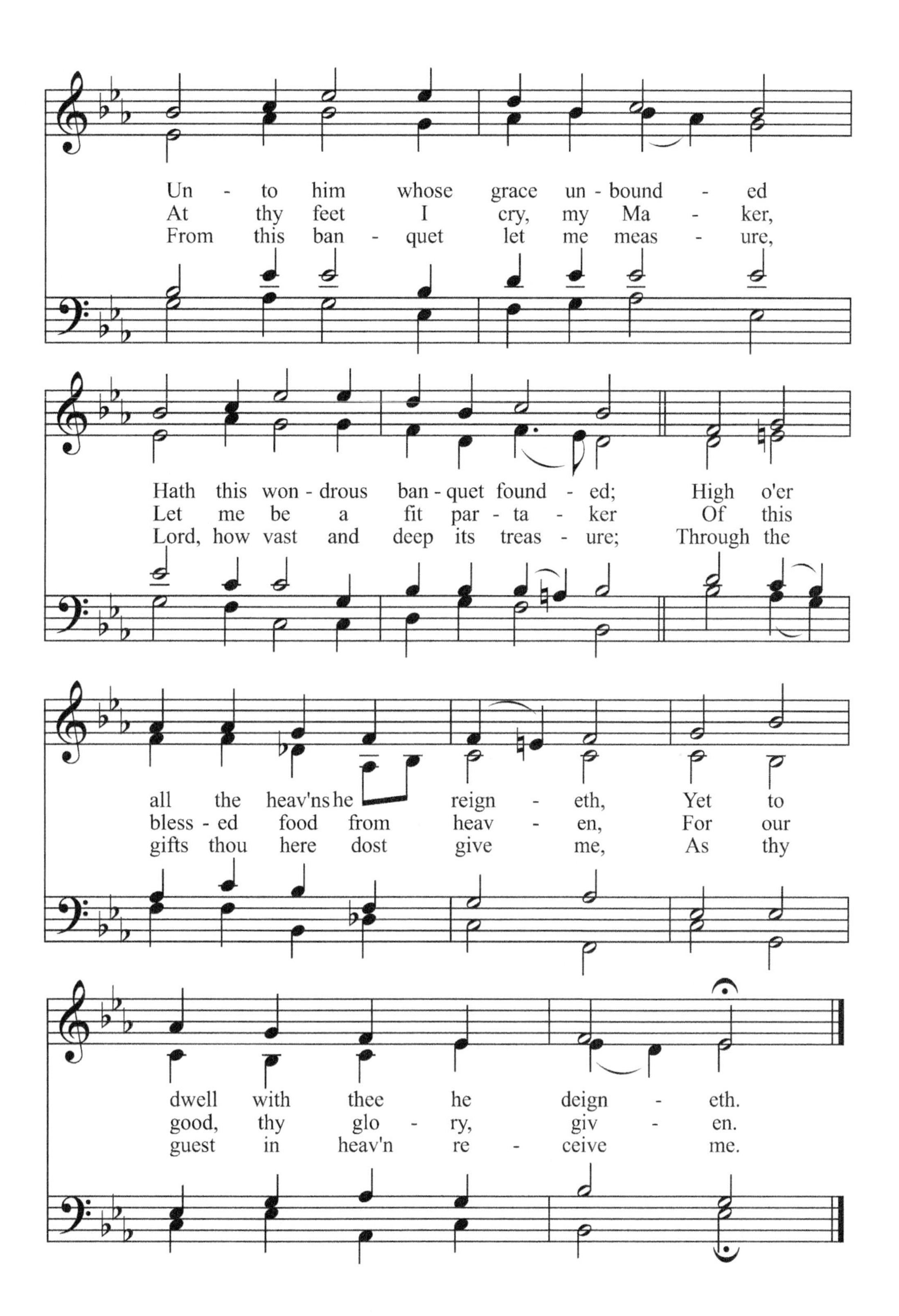
Un - to him whose grace un - bound - ed
At thy feet I cry, my Ma - ker,
From this ban - quet let me meas - ure,
Hath this won - drous ban - quet found - ed; High o'er
Let me be a fit par - ta - ker Of this
Lord, how vast and deep its treas - ure; Through the
all the heav'ns he reign - eth, Yet to
bless - ed food from heav - en, For our
gifts thou here dost give me, As thy
dwell with thee he deign - eth.
good, thy glo - ry, giv - en.
guest in heav'n re - ceive me.

DRAW NIGH AND TAKE THE BODY

SONG FOUR 10. 10. 10. 10. ORLANDO GIBBONS
BANGOR ANTIPHONER

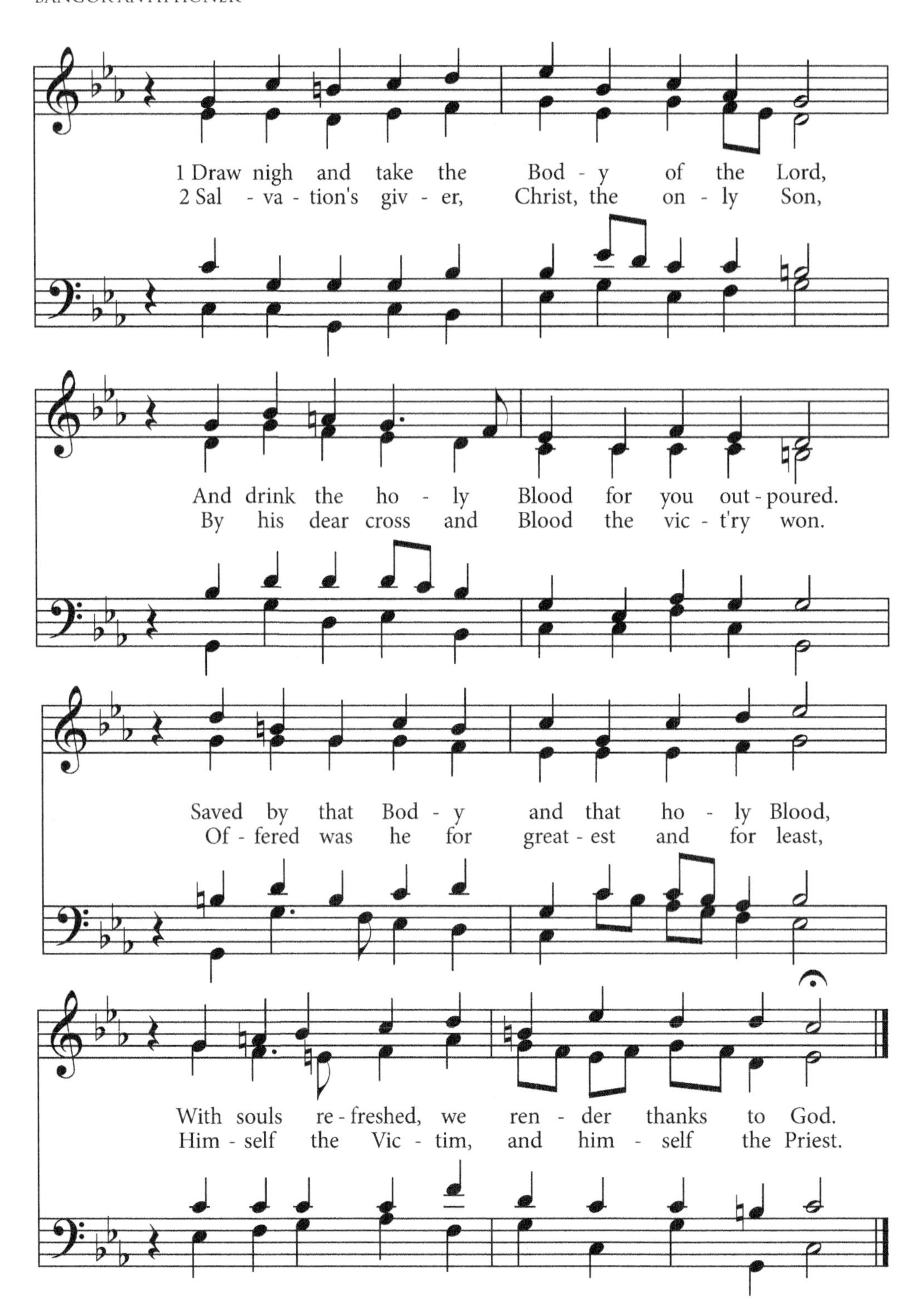

1 Draw nigh and take the Body of the Lord,
And drink the holy Blood for you out-poured.
Saved by that Body and that holy Blood,
With souls refreshed, we render thanks to God.

2 Salvation's giver, Christ, the only Son,
By his dear cross and Blood the vict'ry won.
Offered was he for greatest and for least,
Himself the Victim, and himself the Priest.

DROP, DROP, SLOW TEARS

SONG FORTY-SIX 10. 10. ORLANDO GIBBONS
PHINEAS FLETCHER

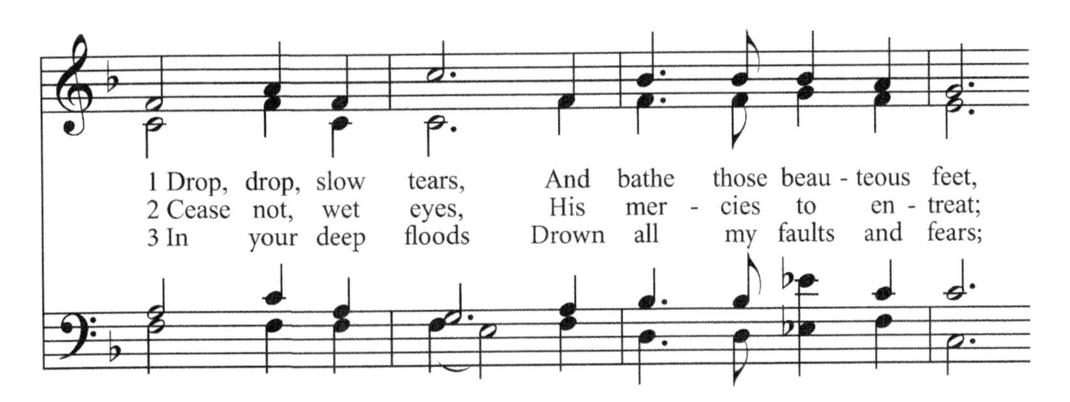

1 Drop, drop, slow tears, And bathe those beau-teous feet,
2 Cease not, wet eyes, His mer-cies to en-treat;
3 In your deep floods Drown all my faults and fears;

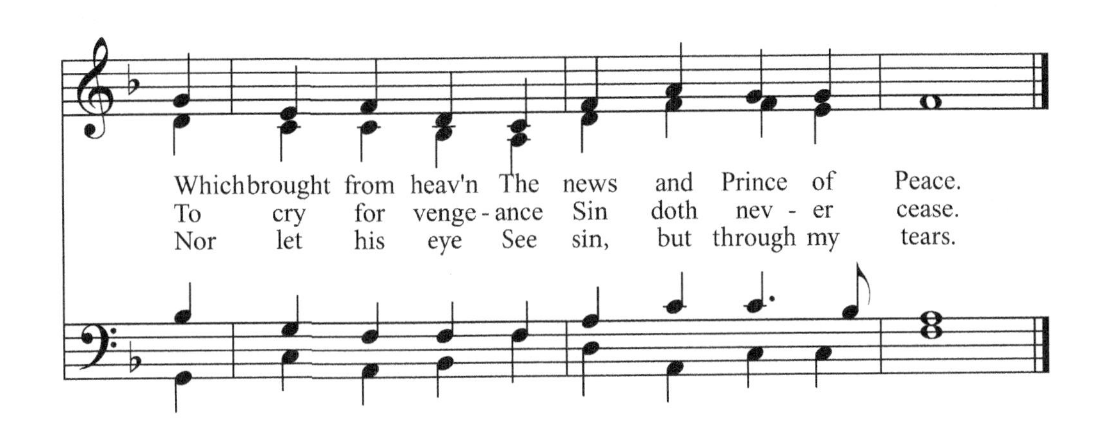

Which brought from heav'n The news and Prince of Peace.
To cry for venge-ance Sin doth nev-er cease.
Nor let his eye See sin, but through my tears.

HAIL! THOU LIVING BREAD

ZIMMERMAN 87. 87.
OLD GERMAN CHORALE

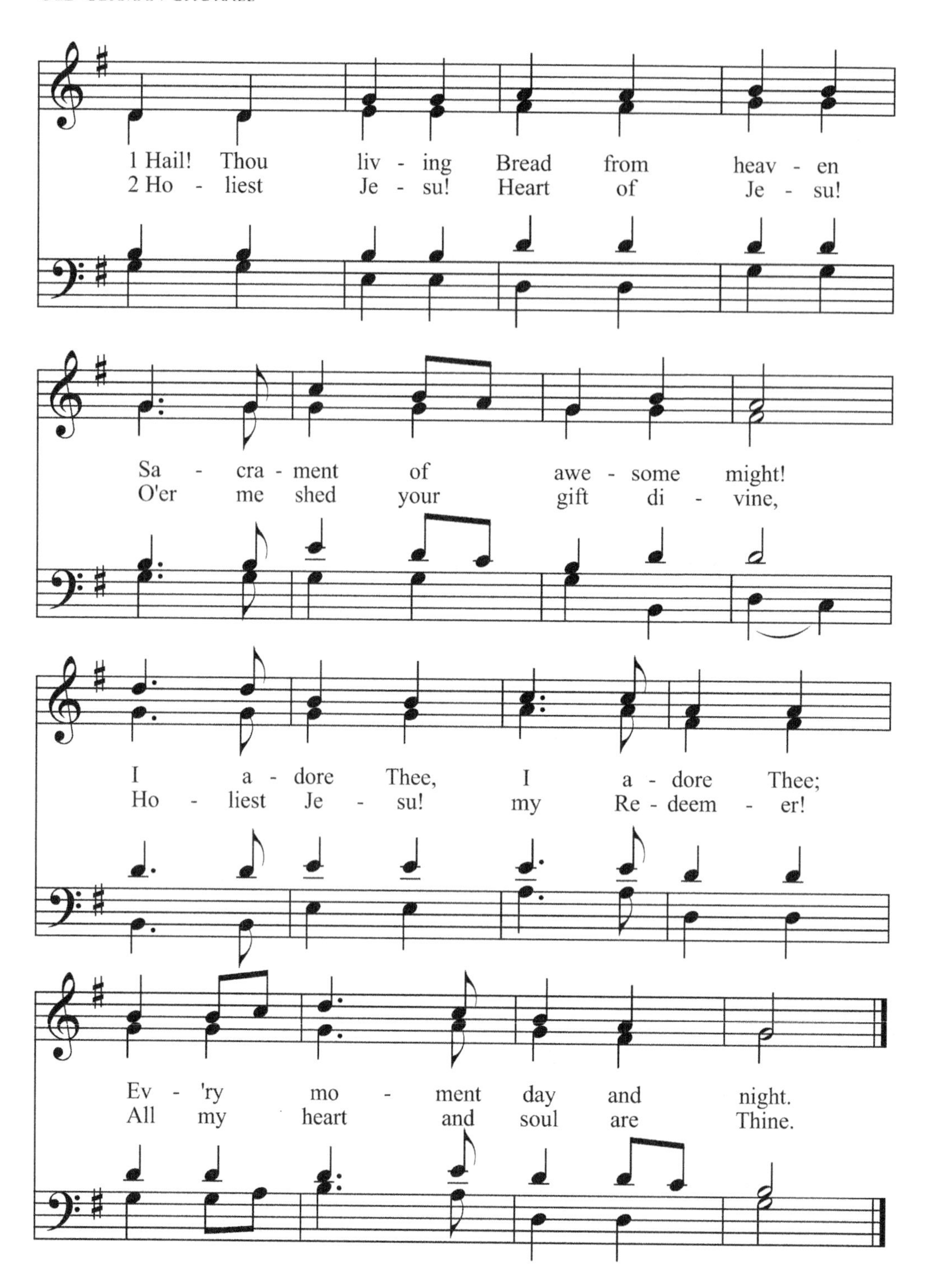

1 Hail! Thou living Bread from heaven
Sacrament of awesome might!
I adore Thee, I adore Thee;
Ev'ry moment day and night.

2 Holiest Jesu! Heart of Jesu!
O'er me shed your gift divine,
Holiest Jesu! my Redeemer!
All my heart and soul are Thine.

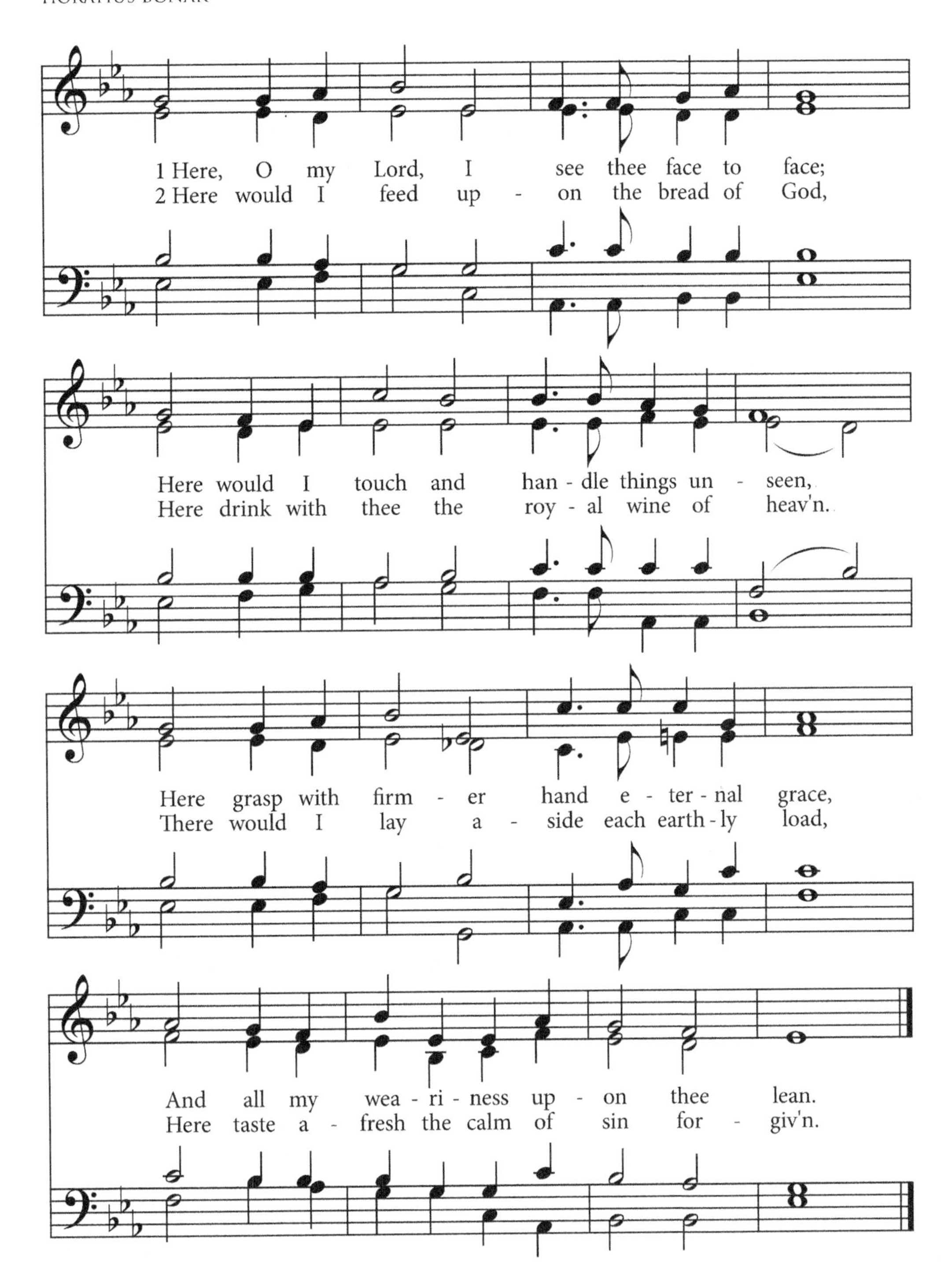

HOLY! HOLY! HOLY! HOLY!

HOFFMAN 8.7.7.5.8.
GERMAN TRADITIONAL

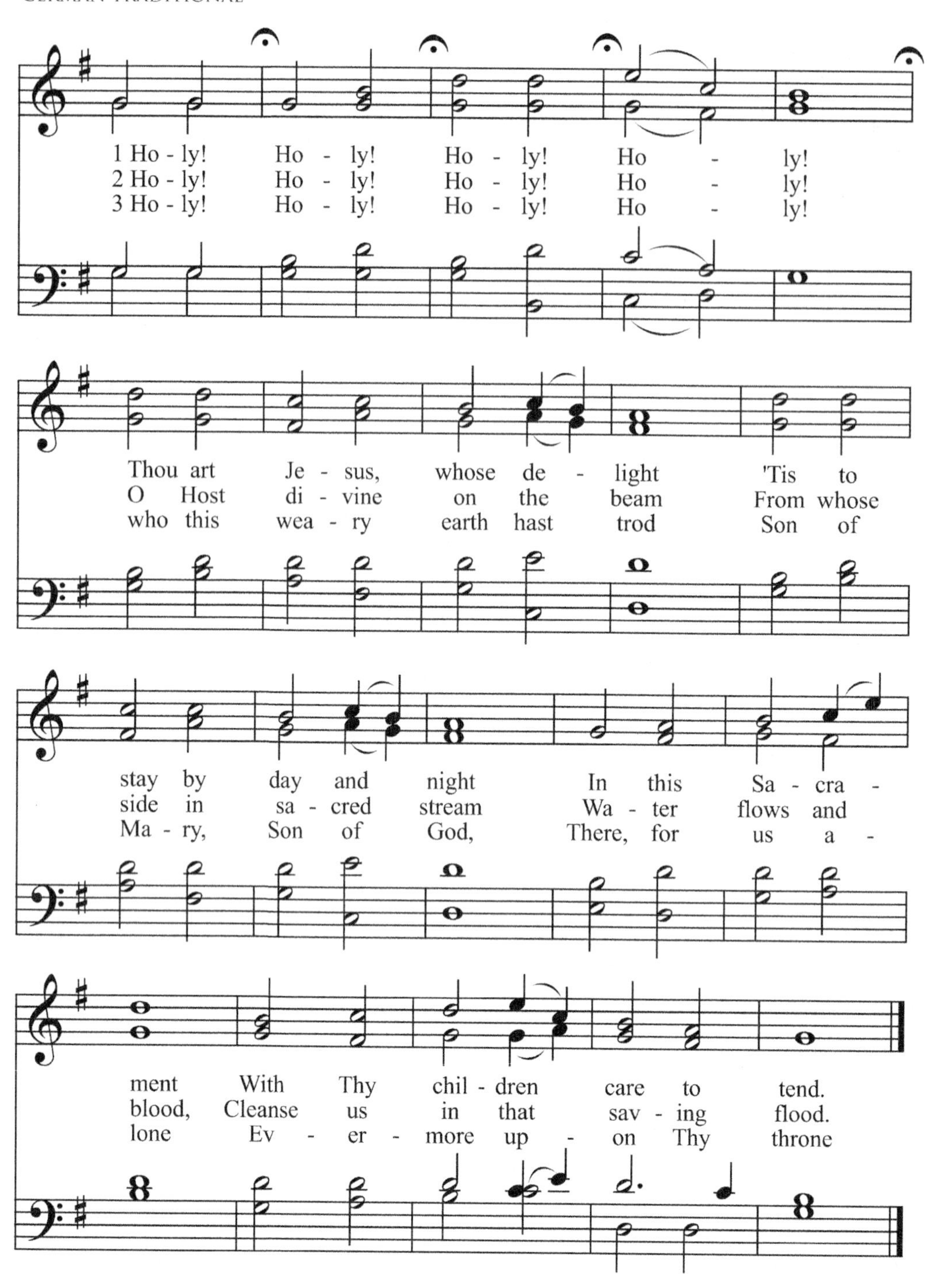

1 Holy! Holy! Holy! Holy! Thou art Jesus, whose delight 'Tis to stay by day and night In this Sacrament With Thy children care to tend.

2 Holy! Holy! Holy! Holy! O Host divine on the beam From whose side in sacred stream Water flows and blood, Cleanse us in that saving flood.

3 Holy! Holy! Holy! Holy! Who this weary earth hast trod Son of Mary, Son of God, There, for us alone Evermore upon Thy throne

IN THIS SACRAMENT, SWEET JESUS

PARTRIDGE 87. 87. 87. 87. HARM. ©2009 NOEL JONES
ANONYMOUS

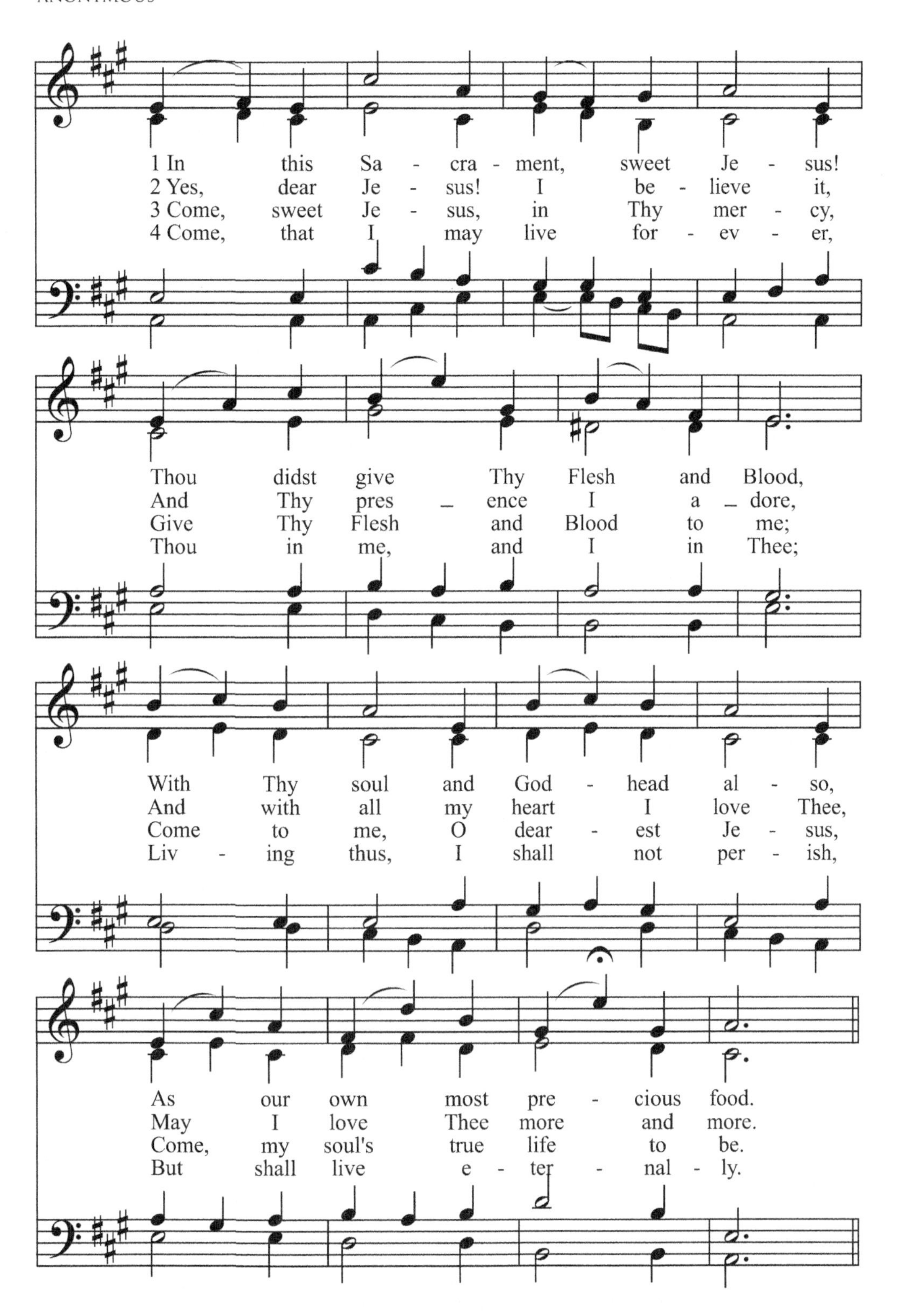

1 In this Sacrament, sweet Jesus! / Thou didst give Thy Flesh and Blood, / With Thy soul and Godhead also, / As our own most precious food.

2 Yes, dear Jesus! I believe it, / And Thy presence I adore, / And with all my heart I love Thee, / May I love Thee more and more.

3 Come, sweet Jesus, in Thy mercy, / Give Thy Flesh and Blood to me; / Come to me, O dearest Jesus, / Come, my soul's true life to be.

4 Come, that I may live forever, / Thou in me, and I in Thee; / Living thus, I shall not perish, / But shall live eternally.

13

IN THIS SACRAMENT, SWEET JESUS

BEAUCHAMP 87. 87. 87. 87.

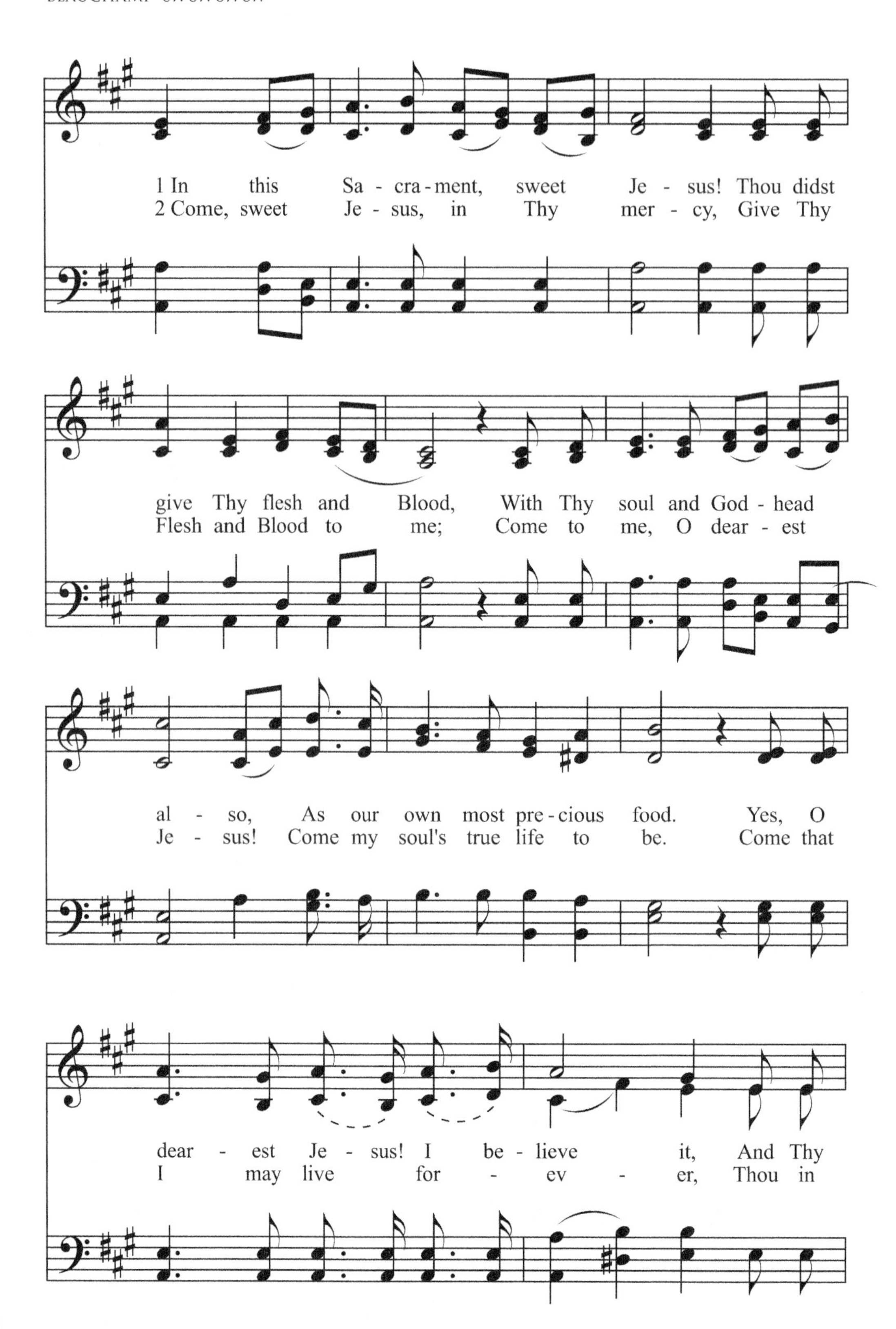

1 In this Sa-cra-ment, sweet Je-sus! Thou didst give Thy flesh and Blood, With Thy soul and God-head al-so, As our own most pre-cious food. Yes, O dear-est Jesus! I be-lieve it, And Thy

2 Come, sweet Je-sus, in Thy mer-cy, Give Thy Flesh and Blood to me; Come to me, O dear-est Je-sus! Come my soul's true life to be. Come that I may live for-ev-er, Thou in

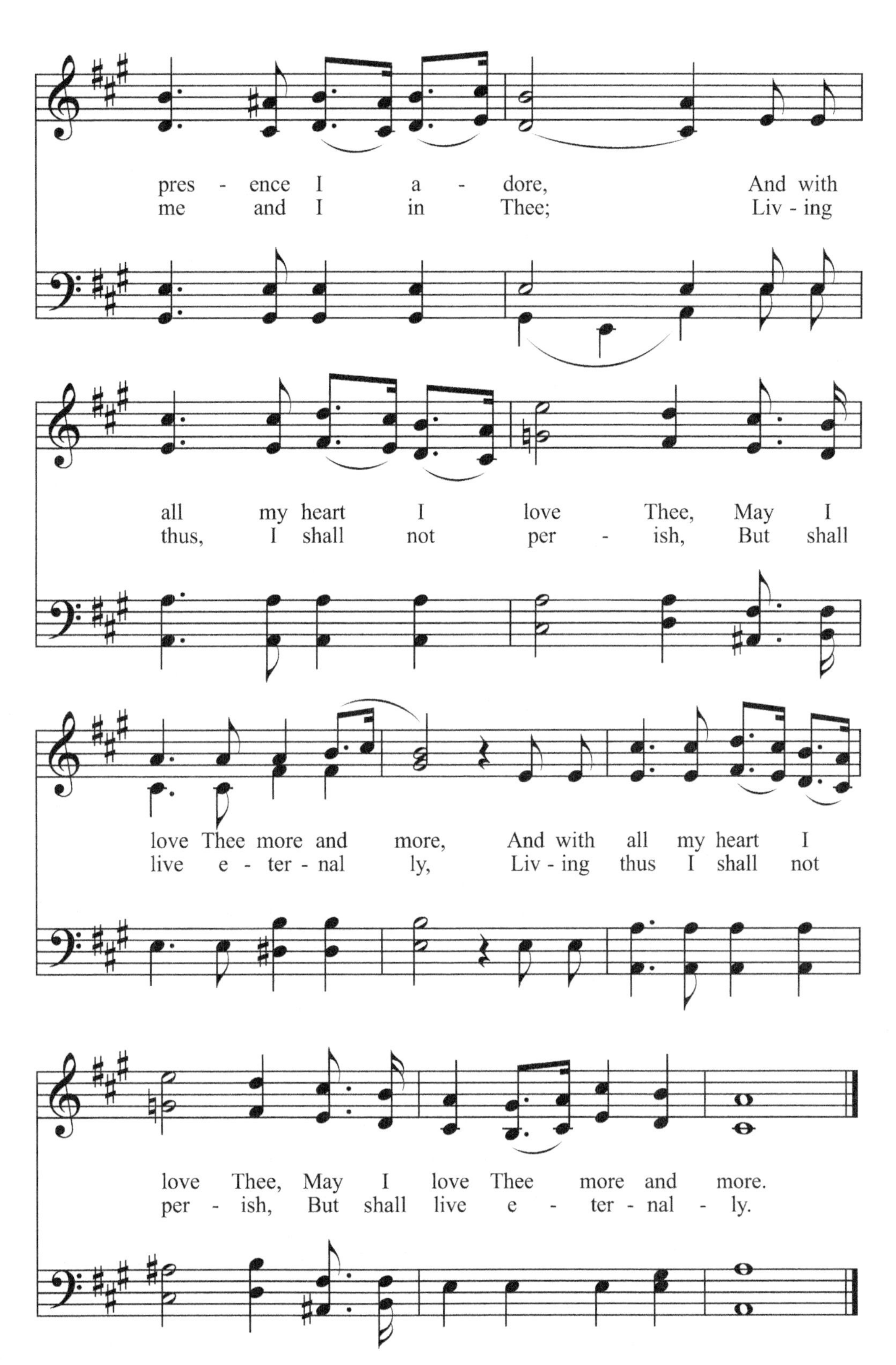
pres - ence I a - dore, And with
me and I in Thee; Liv - ing
all my heart I love Thee, May I
thus, I shall not per - ish, But shall
love Thee more and more, And with all my heart I
live e - ter - nal ly, Liv - ing thus I shall not
love Thee, May I love Thee more and more.
per - ish, But shall live e - ter - nal - ly.

IN THIS SACRAMENT, SWEET JESUS

FAIRBANKS 87. 87. 87. 7.

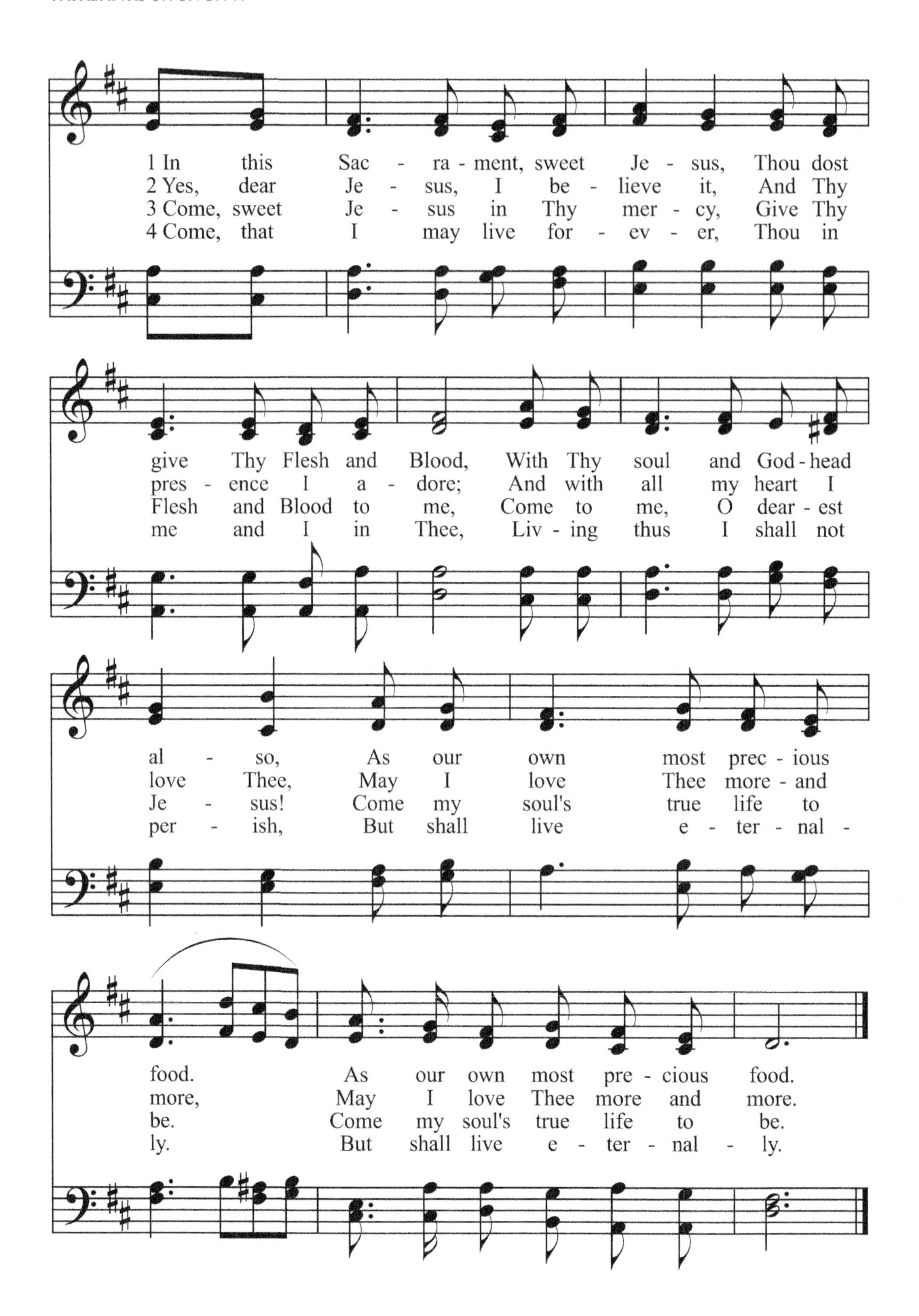

1. In this Sacrament, sweet Jesus, Thou dost give Thy Flesh and Blood, With Thy soul and Godhead also, As our own most precious food. As our own most precious food.

2. Yes, dear Jesus, I believe it, And Thy presence I adore; And with all my heart I love Thee, May I love Thee more and more. May I love Thee more and more.

3. Come, sweet Jesus in Thy mercy, Give Thy Flesh and Blood to me, Come to me, O dearest Jesus! Come my soul's true life to be. Come my soul's true life to be.

4. Come, that I may live forever, Thou in me and I in Thee, Living thus I shall not perish, But shall live eternally. But shall live eternally.

JESUS, FOOD OF ANGELS

INVITATION 65. 65. D CHARLES GOUNOD HARM. ©2009 MARK WINCHESTER
"PARTENDO DAL MONDO"

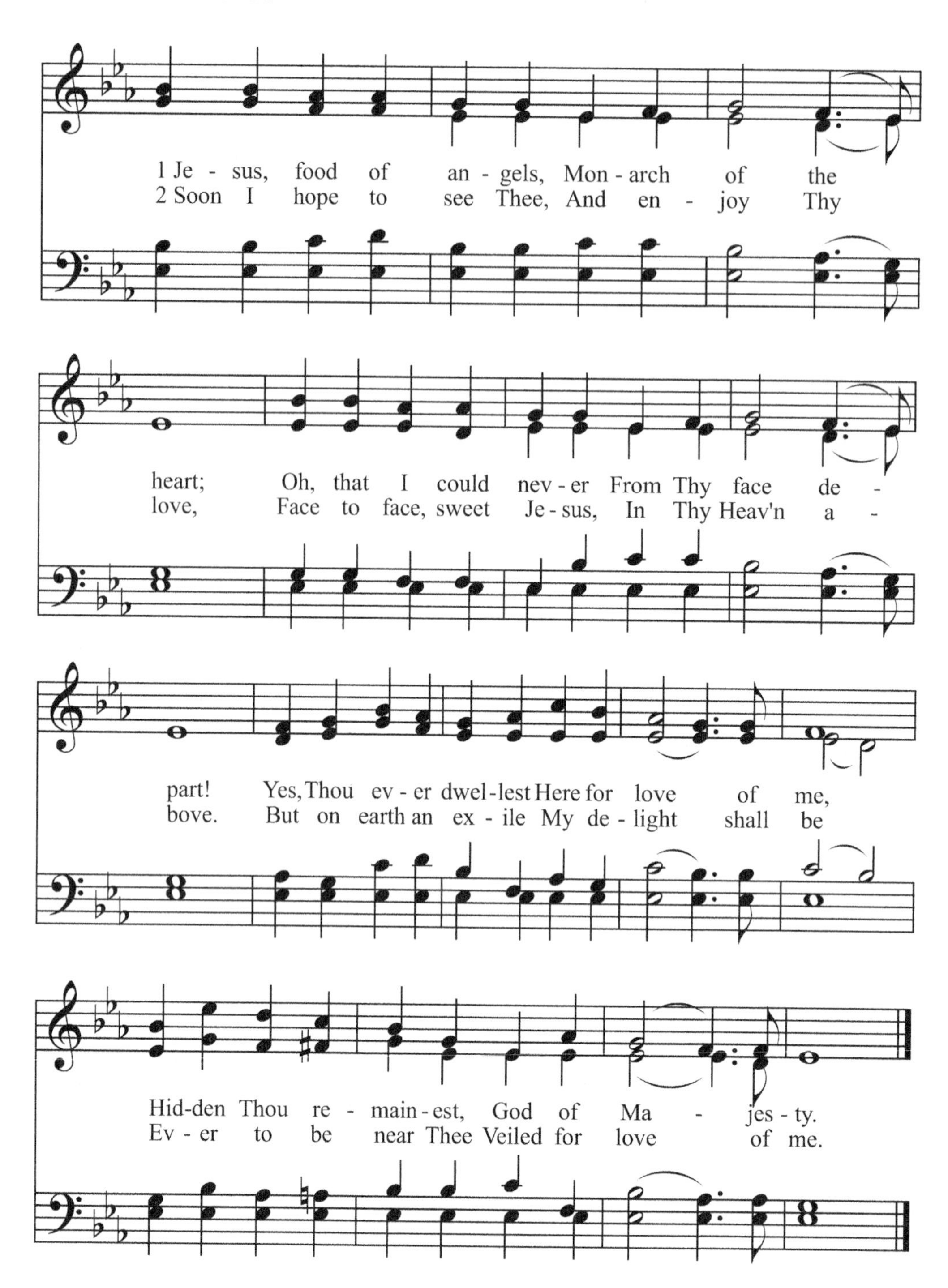

1 Jesus, food of angels, Monarch of the heart; Oh, that I could never From Thy face depart! Yes, Thou ever dwellest Here for love of me, Hidden Thou remainest, God of Majesty.

2 Soon I hope to see Thee, And enjoy Thy love, Face to face, sweet Jesus, In Thy Heav'n above. But on earth an exile My delight shall be Ever to be near Thee Veiled for love of me.

JESUS, FOOD OF ANGELS

HOMAGE 65. 65. D   C. ETT
Vs 1,2 ST. ALPHONSUS Vs. 3 ST. THOMAS AQUINAS

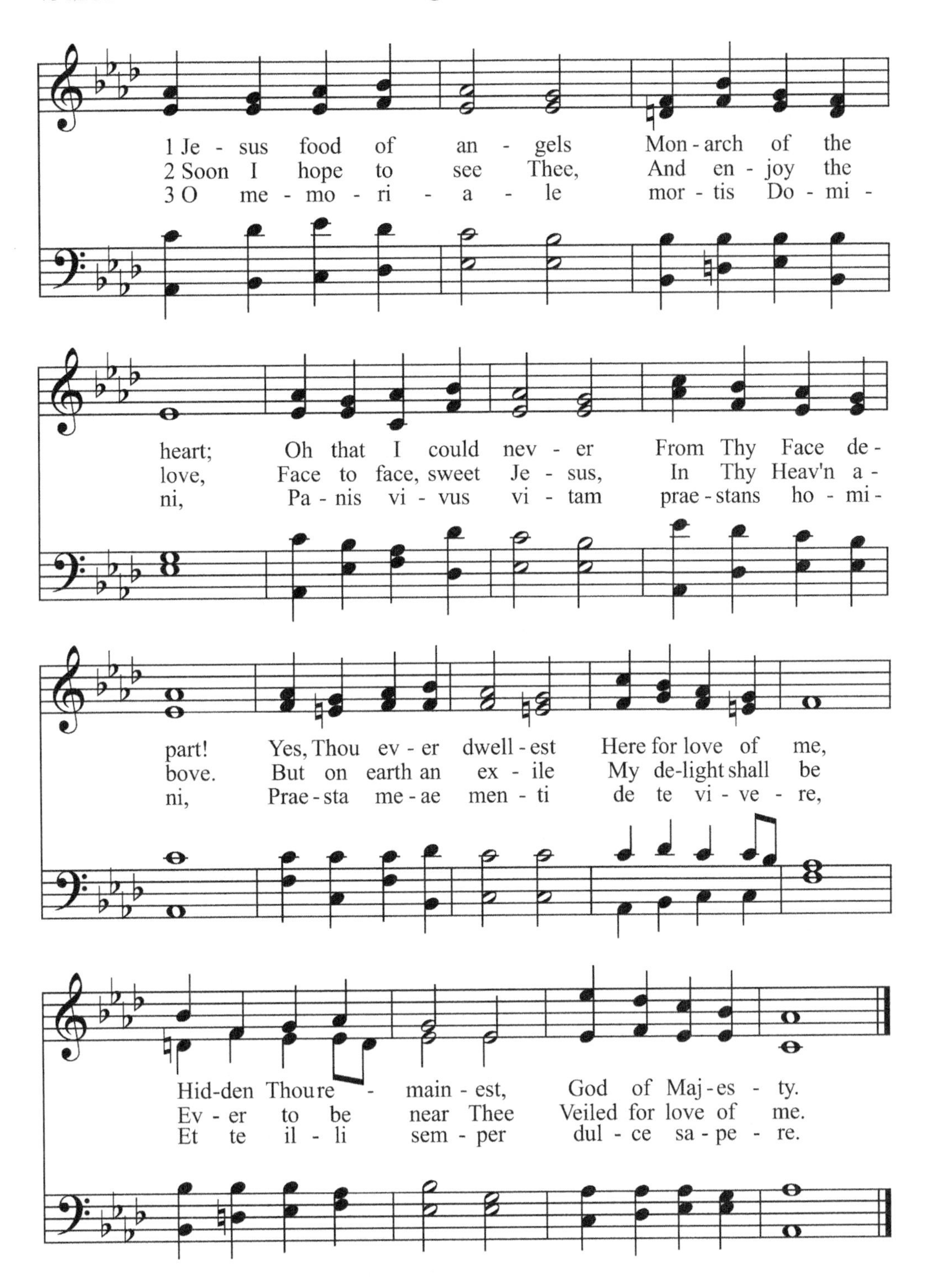

1 Jesus food of angels Monarch of the heart; Oh that I could never From Thy Face depart! Yes, Thou ever dwellest Here for love of me, Hidden Thou remainest, God of Majesty.

2 Soon I hope to see Thee, And enjoy the love, Face to face, sweet Jesus, In Thy Heav'n above. But on earth an exile My delight shall be Ever to be near Thee Veiled for love of me.

3 O memoriale mortis Domini, Panis vivus vitam praestans homini, Praesta meae menti de te vivere, Et te illi semper dulce sapere.

JESUS, GENTLEST SAVIOUR

WAKEFIELD 65. 65. D. A. HUEGLE
REV. F. W. FABER

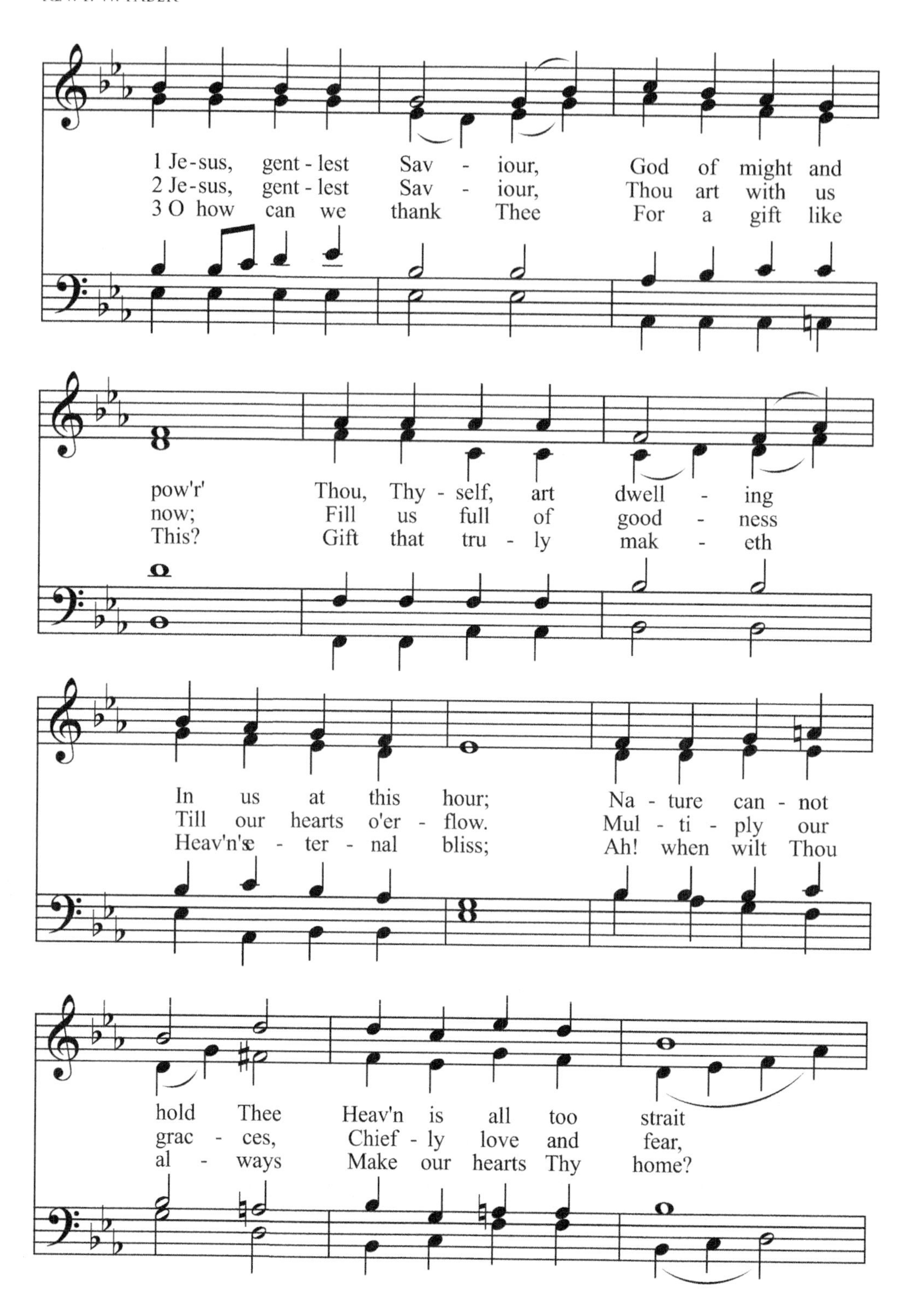

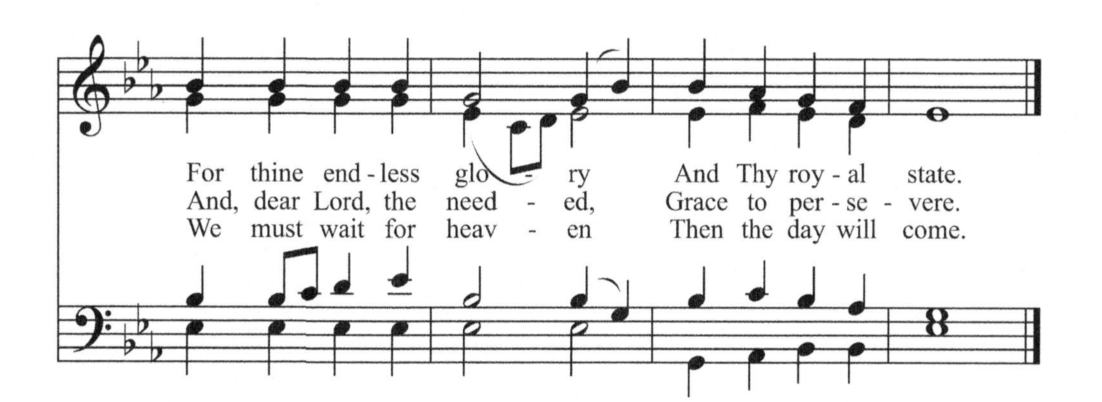

JESUS, GENTLEST SAVIOUR

BEAUMONT 65. 65. N. A. MONTANI HARM. Ï2009 MARK WINCHESTER
REV. F. W. FABER

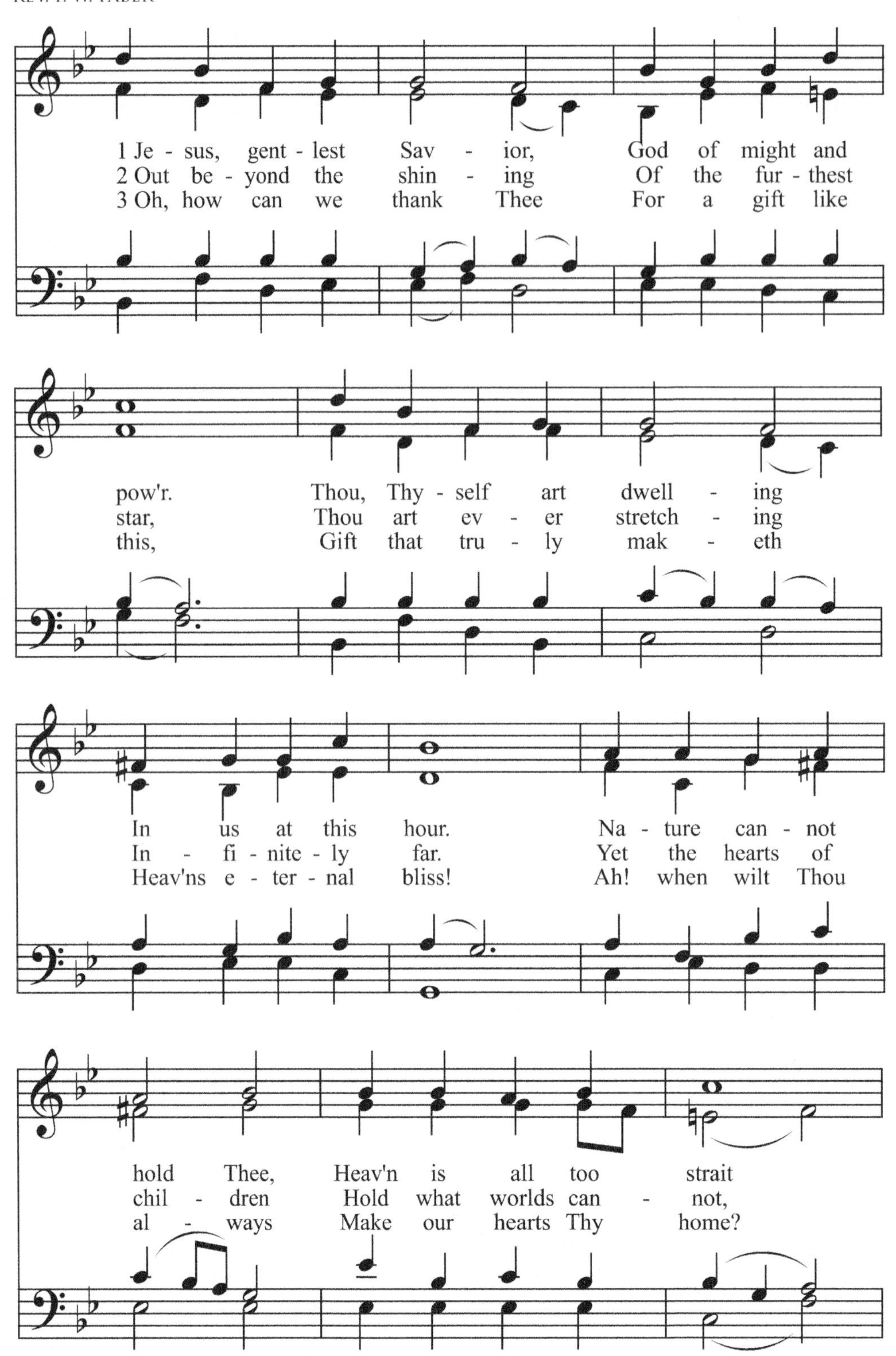

1 Jesus, gentlest Savior, God of might and pow'r. Thou, Thyself art dwelling In us at this hour. Nature cannot hold Thee, Heav'n is all too strait

2 Out beyond the shining Of the furthest star, Thou art ever stretching Infinitely far. Yet the hearts of children Hold what worlds cannot,

3 Oh, how can we thank Thee For a gift like this, Gift that truly maketh Heav'ns eternal bliss! Ah! when wilt Thou always Make our hearts Thy home?

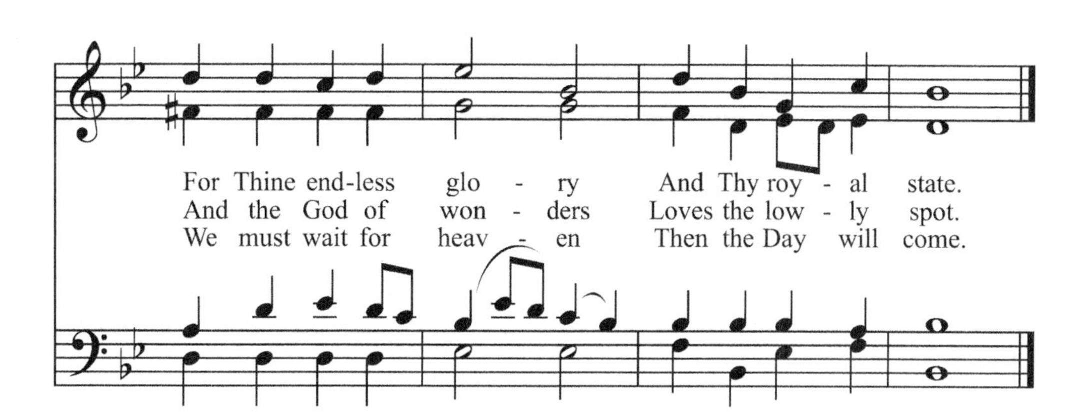
For Thine end-less glo - ry And Thy roy - al state.
And the God of won - ders Loves the low - ly spot.
We must wait for heav - en Then the Day will come.

JESUS, JESUS, COME TO ME

BELVEDERE 77. 77. 77. 77. P. PIEL BASS ©2009 MARK WINCHESTER

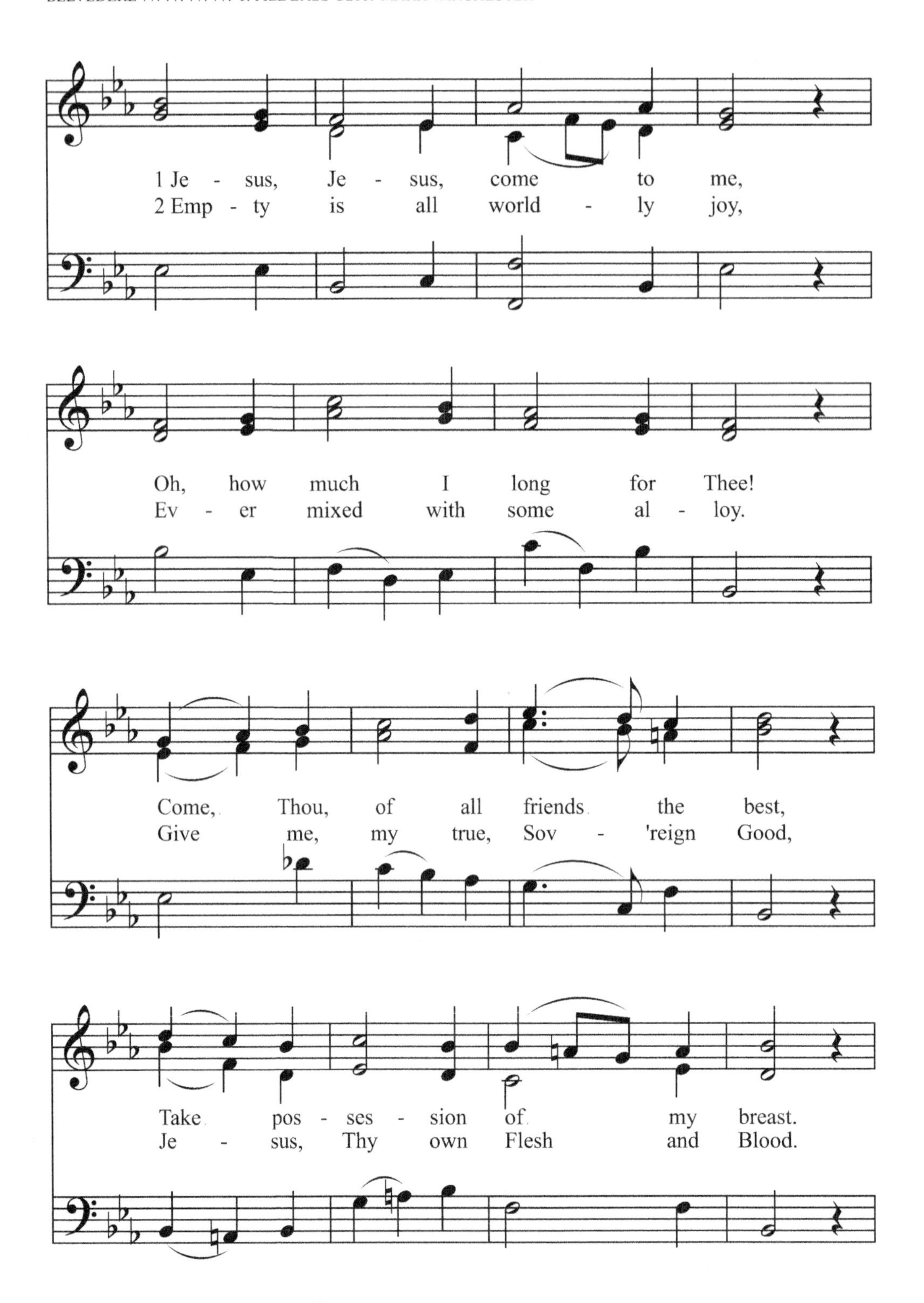

1 Jesus, Jesus, come to me,
Oh, how much I long for Thee!
Come, Thou, of all friends the best,
Take possession of my breast.

2 Empty is all worldly joy,
Ever mixed with some alloy.
Give me, my true, Sov'reign Good,
Jesus, Thy own Flesh and Blood.

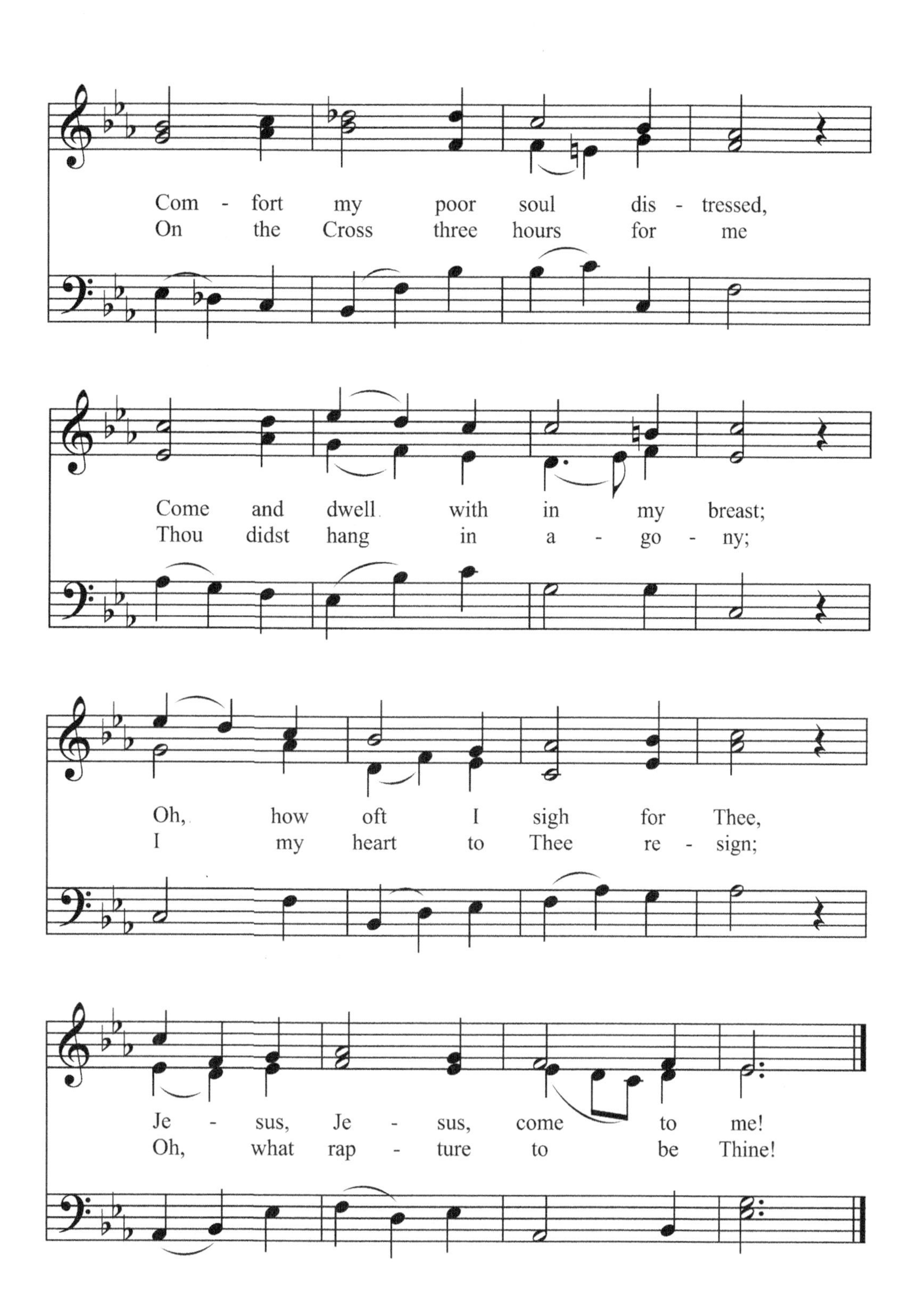
Com - fort my poor soul dis - tressed,
On the Cross three hours for me
Come and dwell with in my breast;
Thou didst hang in a - go - ny;
Oh, how oft I sigh for Thee,
I my heart to Thee re - sign;
Je - sus, Je - sus, come to me!
Oh, what rap - ture to be Thine!

JESUS, JESUS, COME TO ME

MERBECKE 77. 77. HARM. ©2009 MARK WINCHESTER

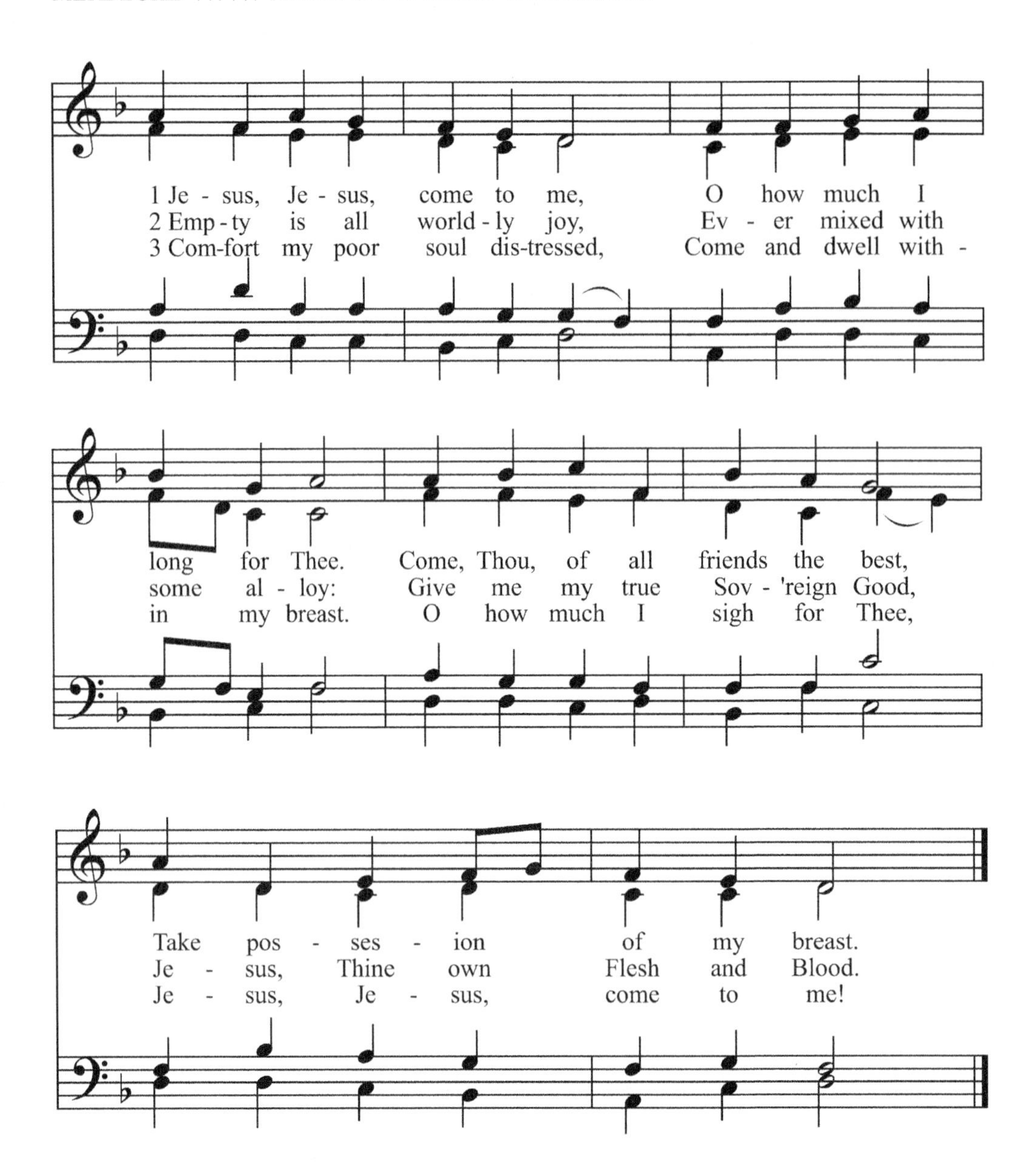

1. Jesus, Jesus, come to me, O how much I long for Thee. Come, Thou, of all friends the best, Take possesion of my breast.
2. Empty is all worldly joy, Ever mixed with some alloy: Give me my true Sov'reign Good, Jesus, Thine own Flesh and Blood.
3. Comfort my poor soul distressed, Come and dwell within my breast. O how much I sigh for Thee, Jesus, Jesus, come to me!

JESUS, LORD, BE THOU MY OWN

CHADWICK 77. 77.

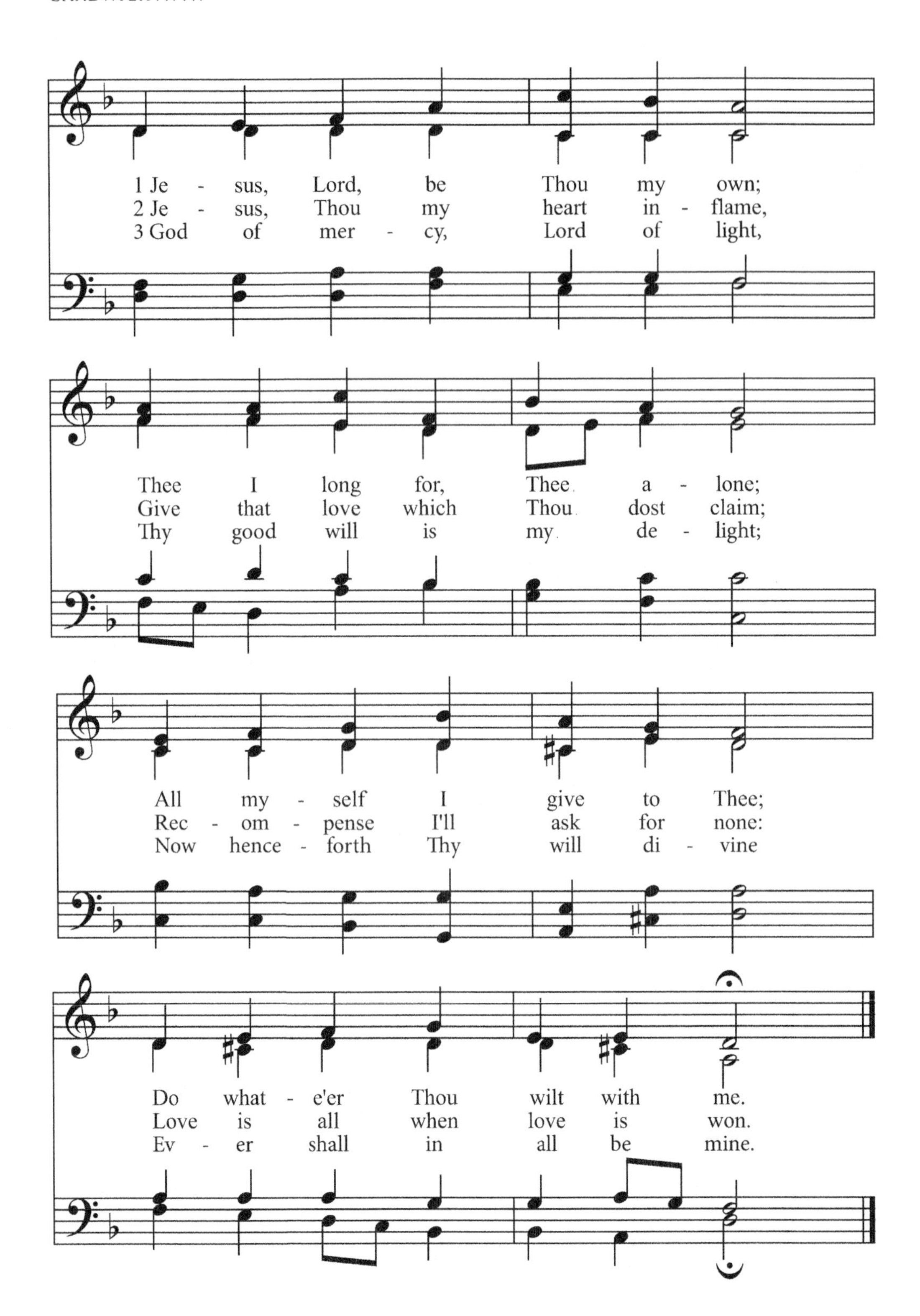

1 Jesus, Lord, be Thou my own;
Thee I long for, Thee alone;
All myself I give to Thee;
Do what-e'er Thou wilt with me.

2 Jesus, Thou my heart inflame,
Give that love which Thou dost claim;
Recompense I'll ask for none:
Love is all when love is won.

3 God of mercy, Lord of light,
Thy good will is my delight;
Now henceforth Thy will divine
Ever shall in all be mine.

JESUS, MY LORD, MY GOD, MY ALL

SWEET SACRAMENT LM WITH REFRAIN
FR. FREDERICK FABER

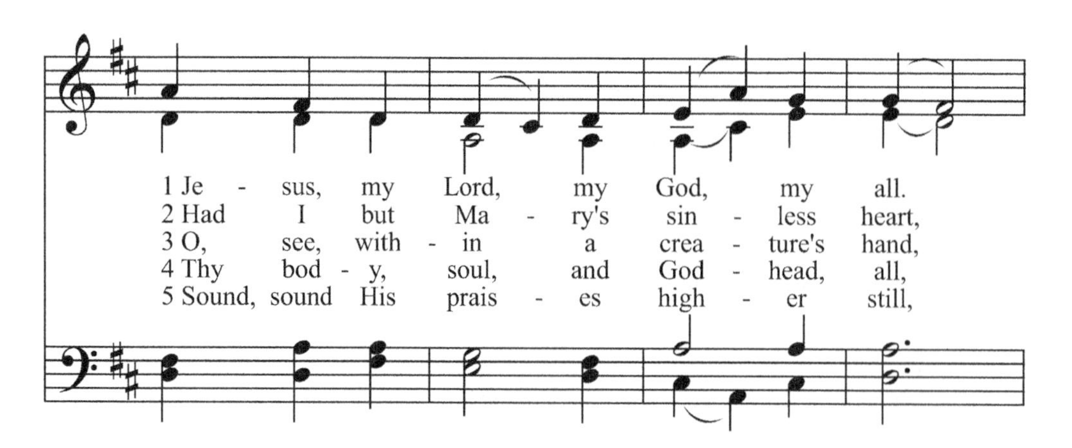

1 Jesus, my Lord, my God, my all.
2 Had I but Mary's sinless heart,
3 O, see, within a creature's hand,
4 Thy body, soul, and Godhead, all,
5 Sound, sound His praises higher still,

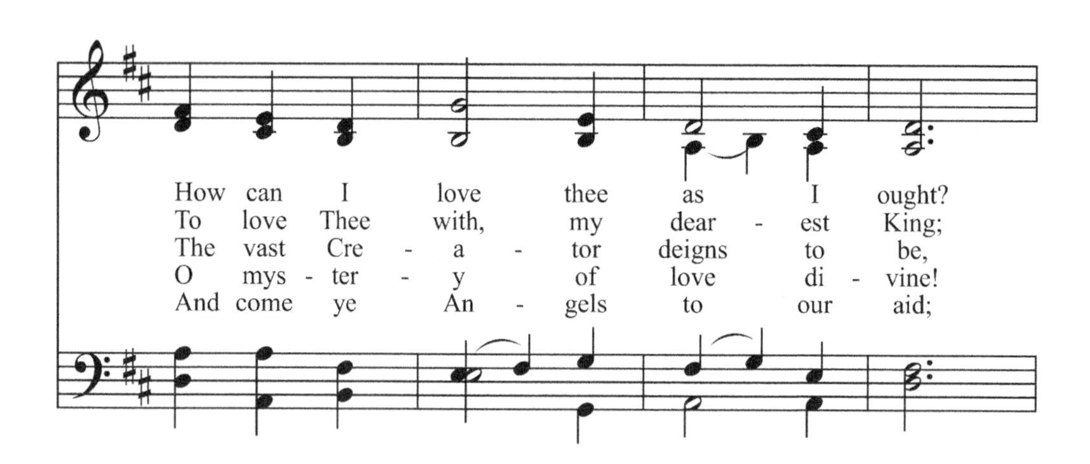

How can I love thee as I ought?
To love Thee with, my dearest King;
The vast Creator deigns to be,
O mystery of love divine!
And come ye Angels to our aid;

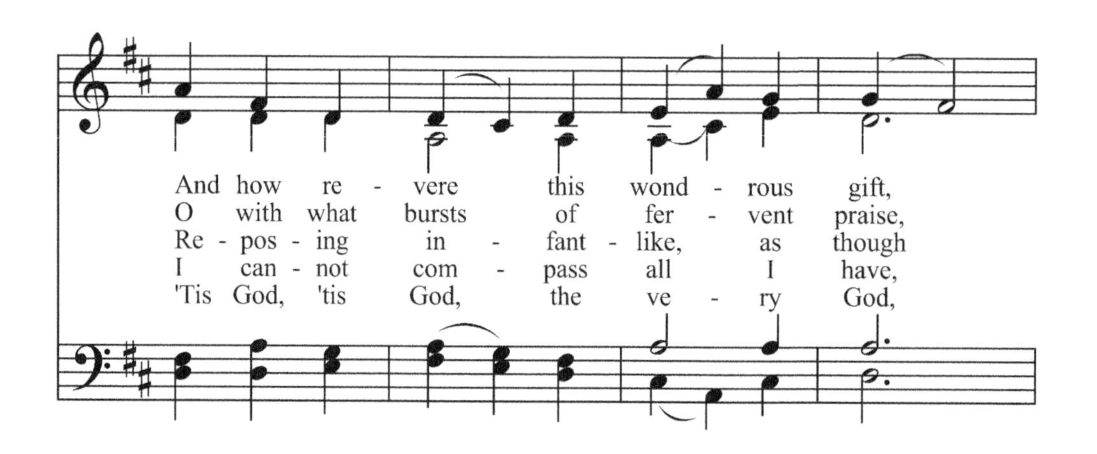

And how revere this wondrous gift,
O with what bursts of fervent praise,
Reposing infant-like, as though
I cannot compass all I have,
'Tis God, 'tis God, the very God,

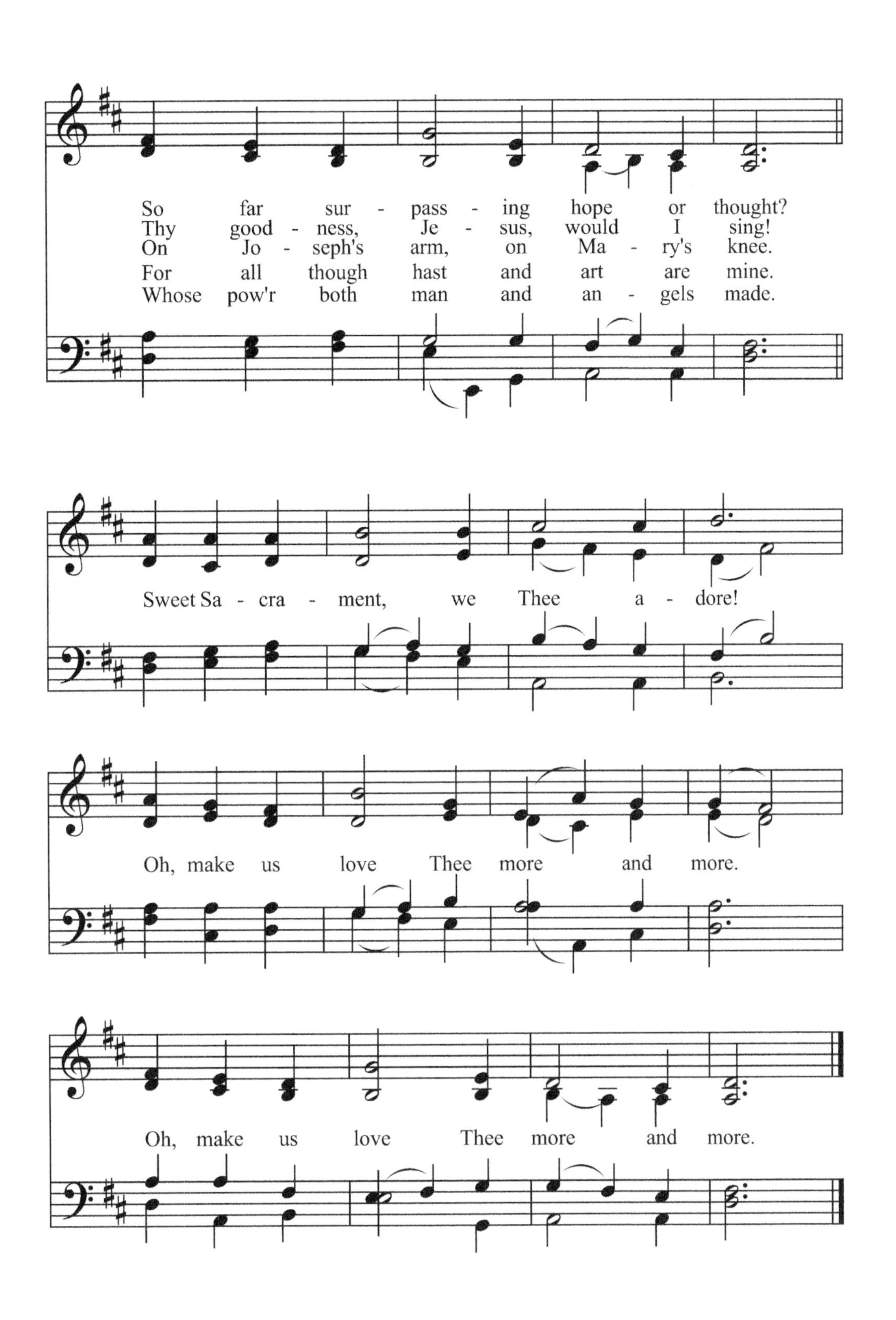
So far surpassing hope or thought?
Thy goodness, Jesus, would I sing!
On Joseph's arm, on Mary's knee.
For all though hast and art are mine.
Whose pow'r both man and angels made.
Sweet Sacrament, we Thee adore!
Oh, make us love Thee more and more.
Oh, make us love Thee more and more.

JESUS, THOU ART COMING

INVITATION 65. 65. D. CHARLES GOUNOD
SR. MARIE XAVIER

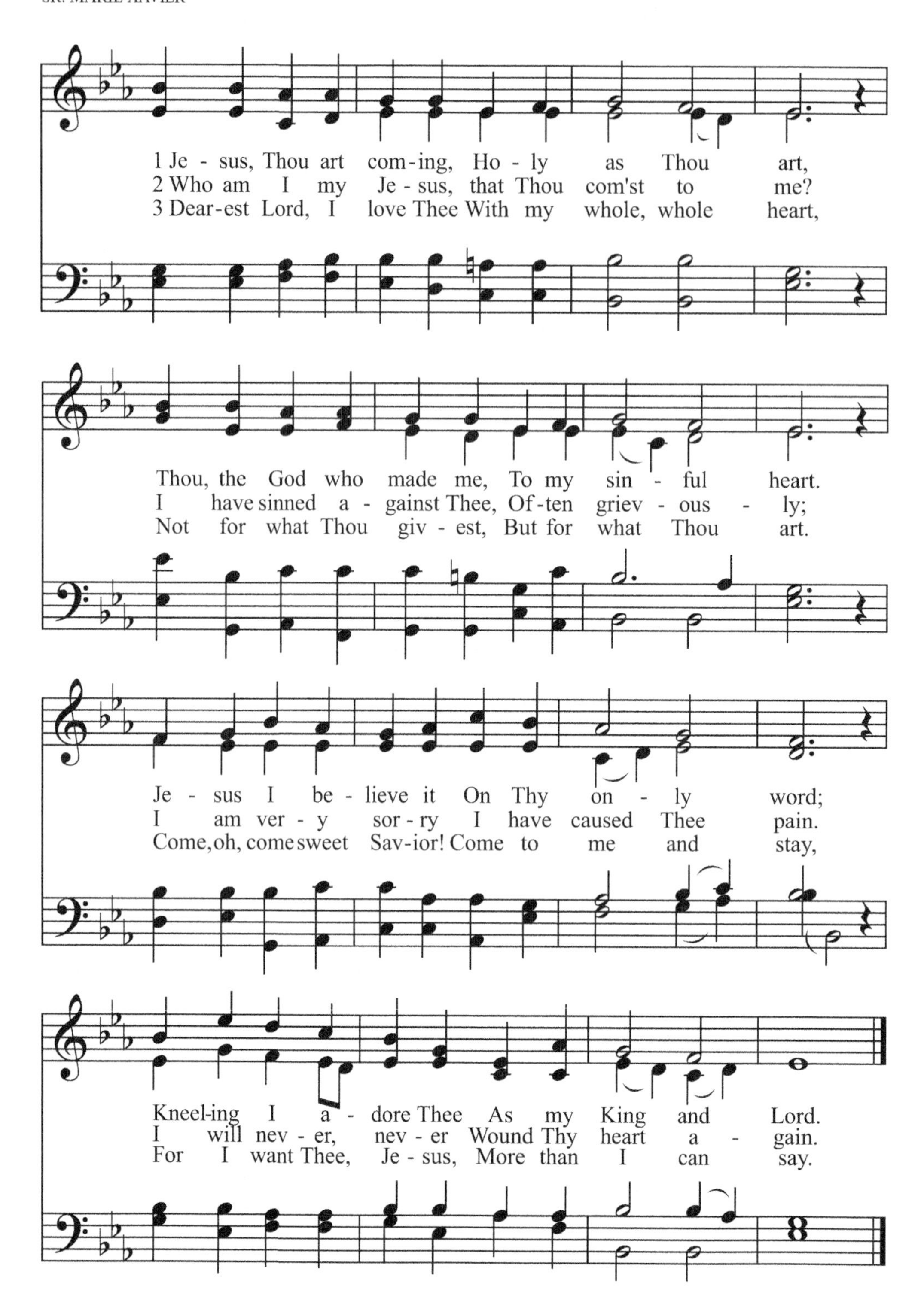

1 Je-sus, Thou art com-ing, Ho-ly as Thou art,
2 Who am I my Je-sus, that Thou com'st to me?
3 Dear-est Lord, I love Thee With my whole, whole heart,

Thou, the God who made me, To my sin-ful heart.
I have sinned a-gainst Thee, Of-ten griev-ous-ly;
Not for what Thou giv-est, But for what Thou art.

Je-sus I be-lieve it On Thy on-ly word;
I am ver-y sor-ry I have caused Thee pain.
Come, oh, come sweet Sav-ior! Come to me and stay,

Kneel-ing I a-dore Thee As my King and Lord.
I will nev-er, nev-er Wound Thy heart a-gain.
For I want Thee, Je-sus, More than I can say.

JESUS, THOU ART COMING

DARBY 65. 65. D.

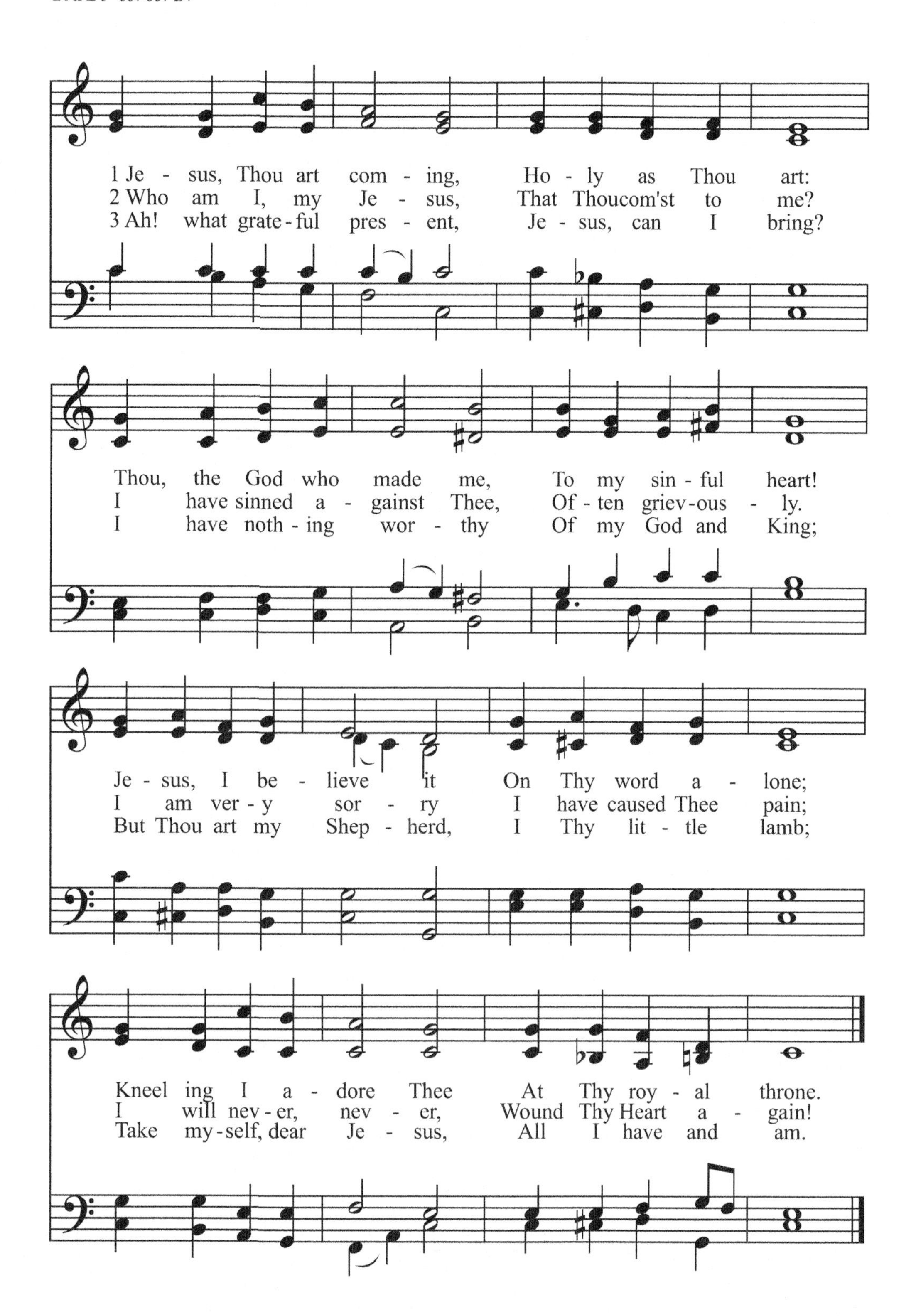

1 Jesus, Thou art coming, Holy as Thou art:
Thou, the God who made me, To my sinful heart!
Jesus, I believe it On Thy word alone;
Kneeling I adore Thee At Thy royal throne.

2 Who am I, my Jesus, That Thou com'st to me?
I have sinned against Thee, Often grievously.
I am very sorry I have caused Thee pain;
I will never, never, Wound Thy Heart again!

3 Ah! what grateful present, Jesus, can I bring?
I have nothing worthy Of my God and King;
But Thou art my Shepherd, I Thy little lamb;
Take myself, dear Jesus, All I have and am.

JESUS, THOU ART COMING

DURAND 65. 65. D.
SR. MARIE XAVIER

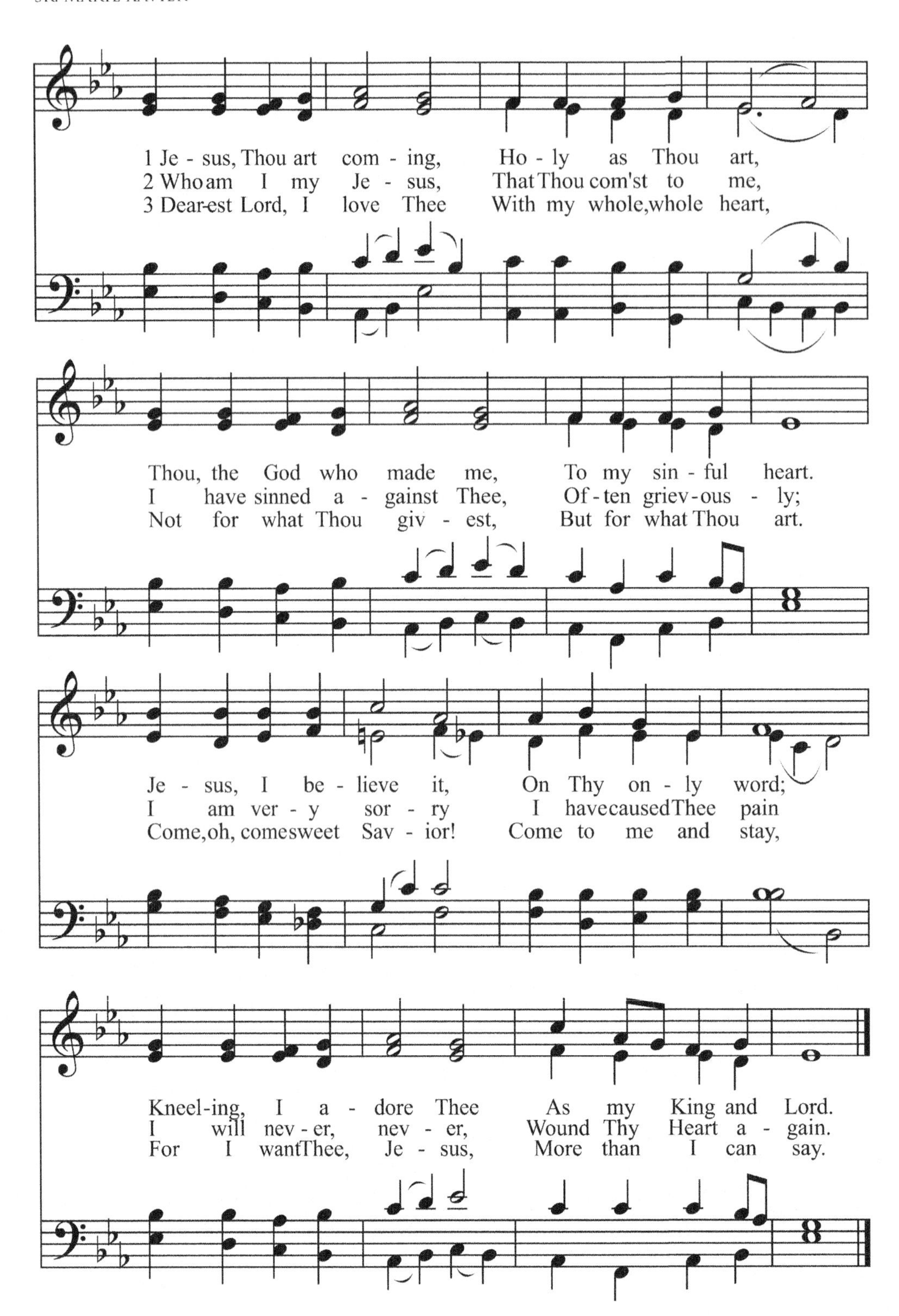

JESUS, THOU ART COMING

DURAND 65. 65. D.
SR. MARIE XAVIER

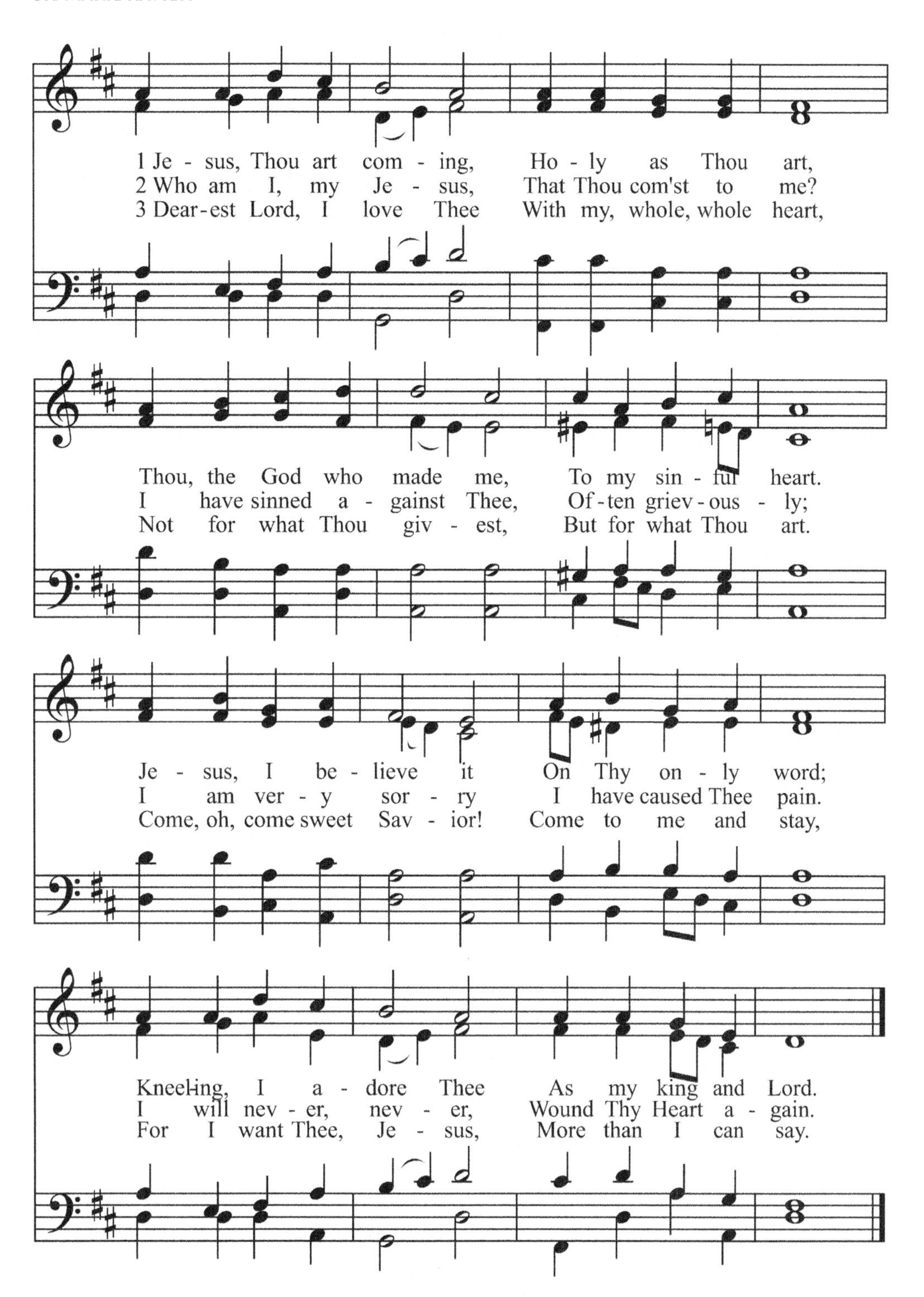

MY GOD, AND IS THY TABLE SPREAD

BEDE 8.8.8.8. NOEL JONES
PHILIP DODDERIDGE

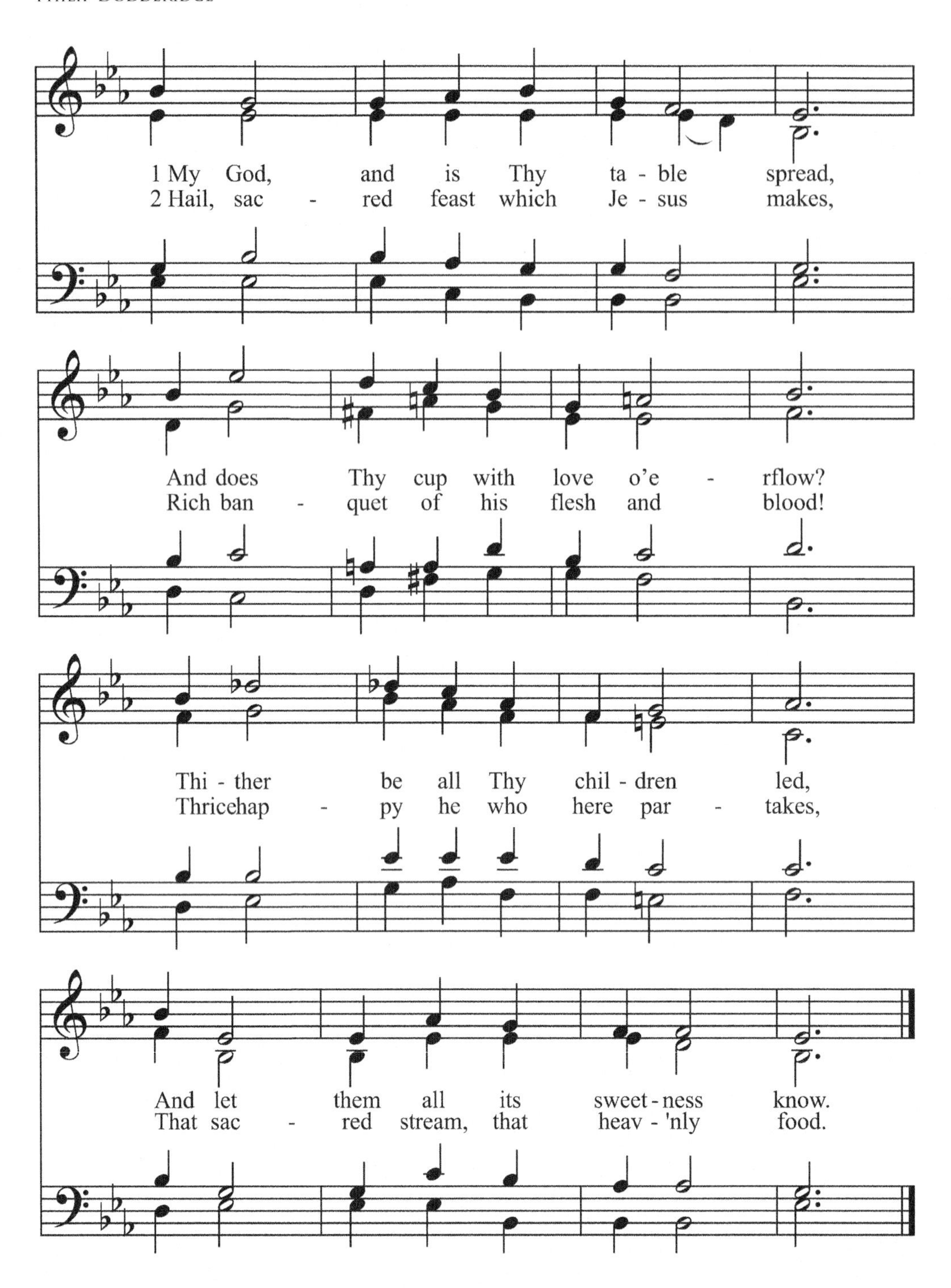

1. My God, and is Thy table spread,
And does Thy cup with love o'erflow?
Thither be all Thy children led,
And let them all its sweetness know.

2. Hail, sacred feast which Jesus makes,
Rich banquet of his flesh and blood!
Thrice happy he who here partakes,
That sacred stream, that heav'nly food.

MY GOD, THY TABLE NOW IS SPREAD

SONG THIRTY-FOUR 88. 88. ORLANDO GIBBONS
PHILIP DODDERIDGE

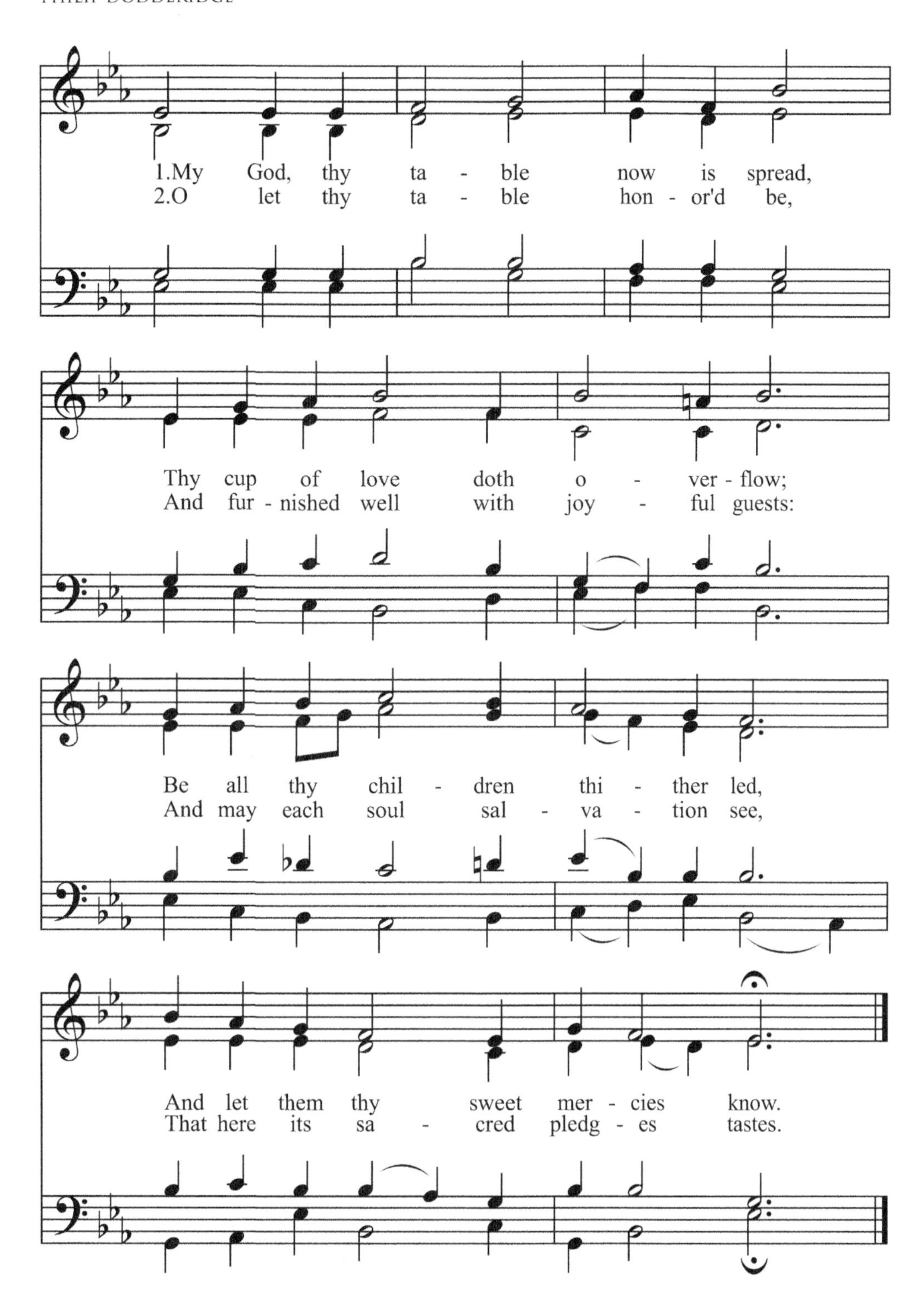

1. My God, thy table now is spread,
Thy cup of love doth o-ver-flow;
Be all thy chil-dren thi-ther led,
And let them thy sweet mer-cies know.

2. O let thy table hon-or'd be,
And fur-nished well with joy-ful guests:
And may each soul sal-va-tion see,
That here its sa-cred pledg-es tastes.

NOW, MY TONGUE, THE MYSTERY

DOWLING 87. 87. 87. NOEL JONES
PANGE LINGUA

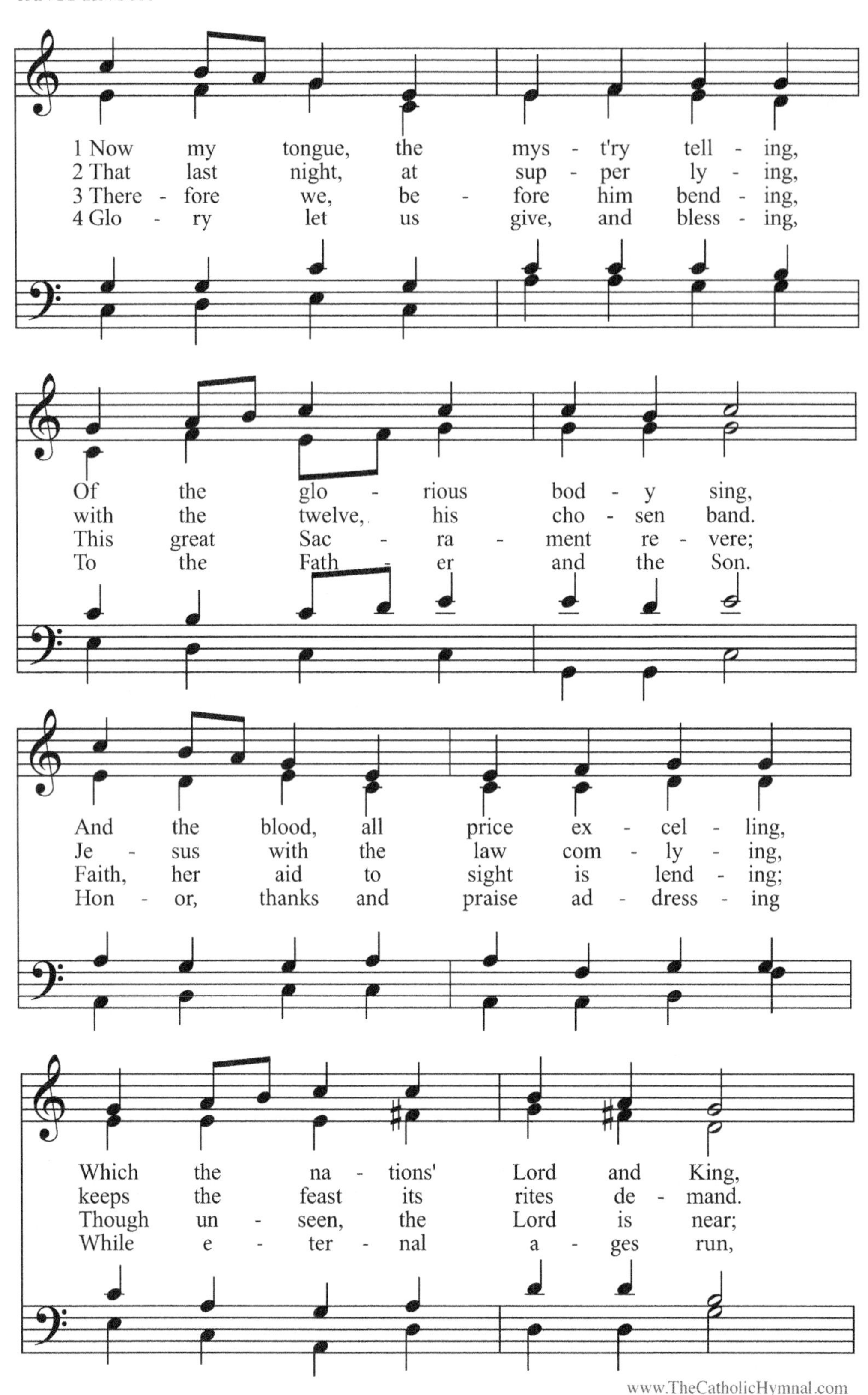

1 Now my tongue, the mys-t'ry tell-ing,
Of the glo-rious bod-y sing,
And the blood, all price ex-cel-ling,
Which the na-tions' Lord and King,

2 That last night, at sup-per ly-ing,
with the twelve, his cho-sen band.
Je-sus with the law com-ply-ing,
keeps the feast its rites de-mand.

3 There-fore we, be-fore him bend-ing,
This great Sac-ra-ment re-vere;
Faith, her aid to sight is lend-ing;
Though un-seen, the Lord is near;

4 Glo-ry let us give, and bless-ing,
To the Fath-er and the Son.
Hon-or, thanks and praise ad-dress-ing
While e-ter-nal a-ges run,

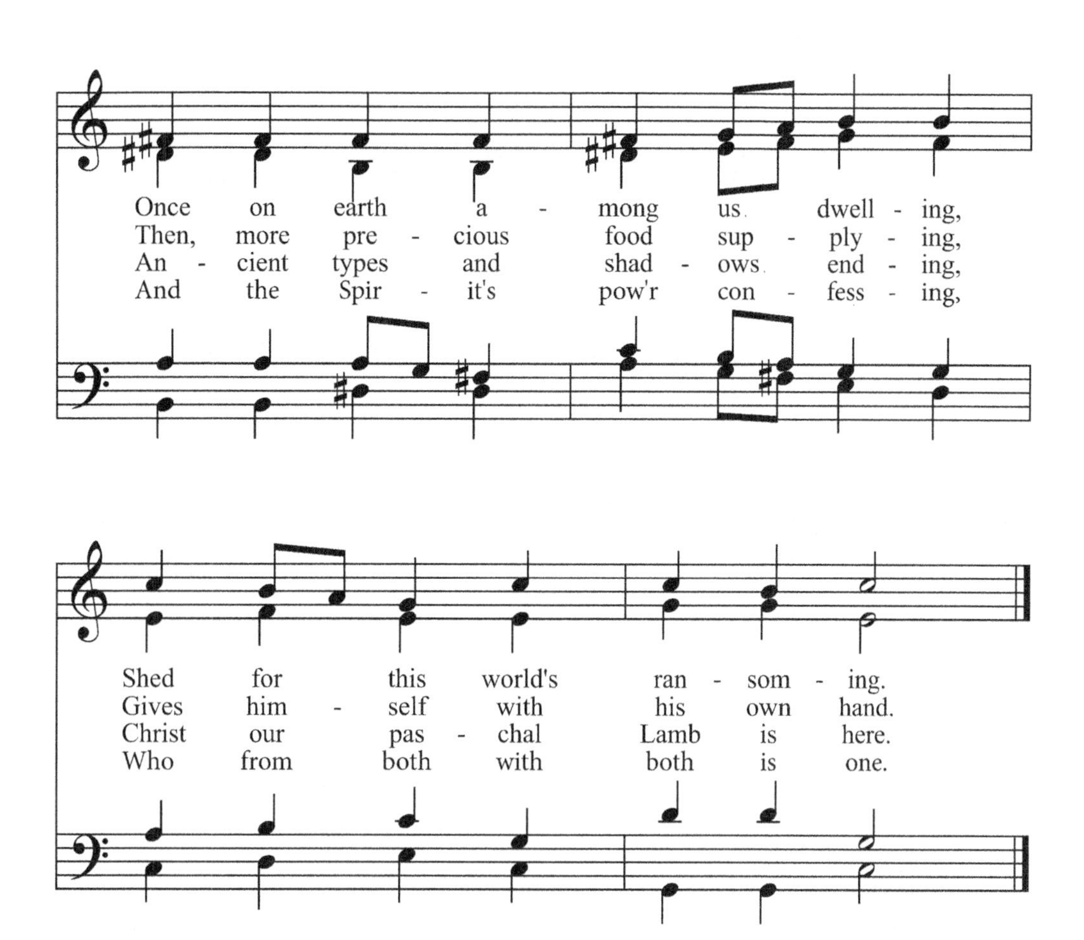
Once on earth a - mong us dwell - ing,
Then, more pre - cious food sup - ply - ing,
An - cient types and shad - ows end - ing,
And the Spir - it's pow'r con - fess - ing,
Shed for this world's ran - som - ing.
Gives him - self with his own hand.
Christ our pas - chal Lamb is here.
Who from both with both is one.

O BREAD OF HEAVEN

SWEET SACRAMENT 88. 88. 88. 88.
ST. ALPHONSUS

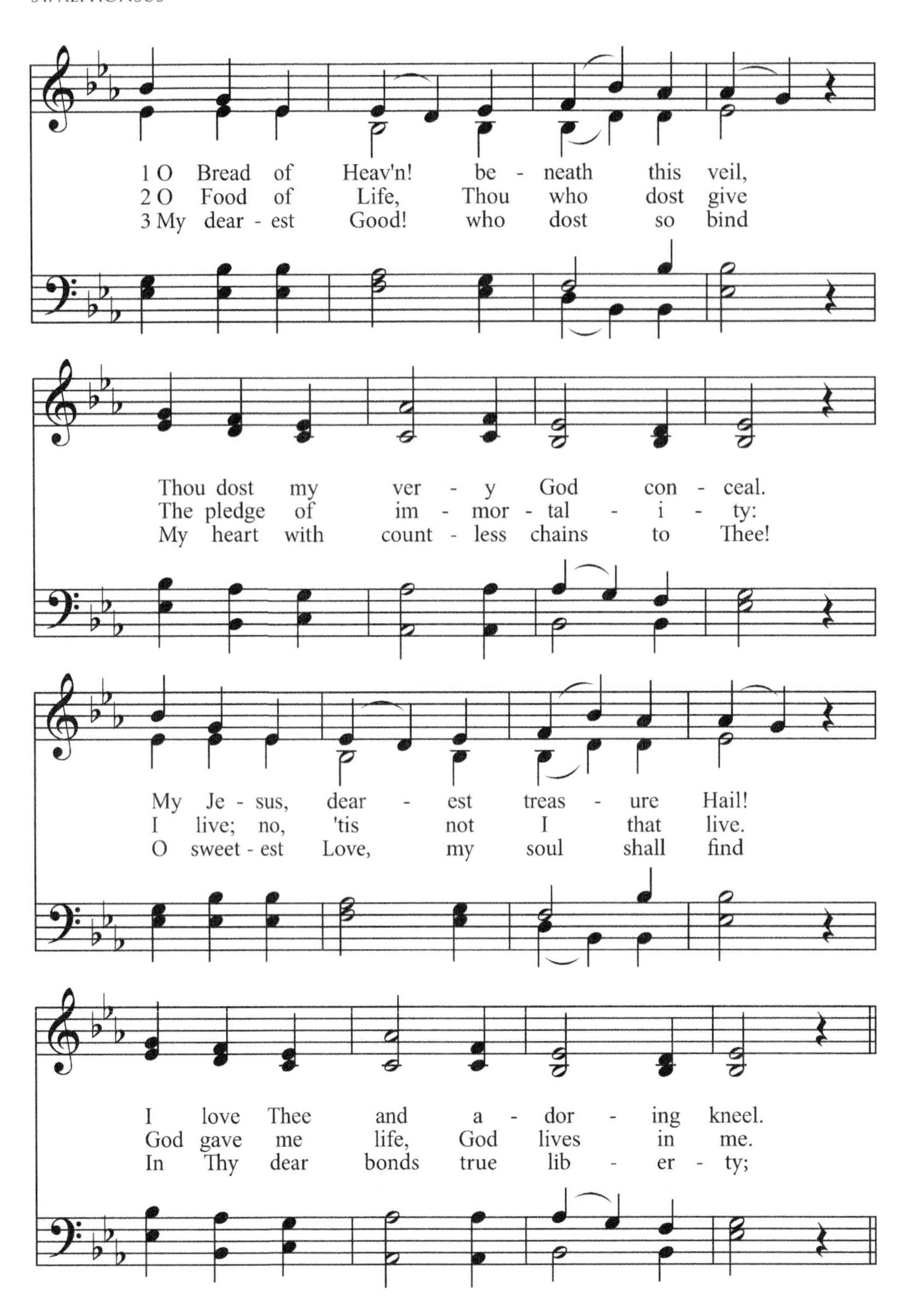

1 O Bread of Heav'n! beneath this veil,
Thou dost my very God conceal.
My Jesus, dearest treasure Hail!
I love Thee and adoring kneel.

2 O Food of Life, Thou who dost give
The pledge of immortality:
I live; no, 'tis not I that live.
God gave me life, God lives in me.

3 My dearest Good! who dost so bind
My heart with countless chains to Thee!
O sweetest Love, my soul shall find
In Thy dear bonds true liberty;

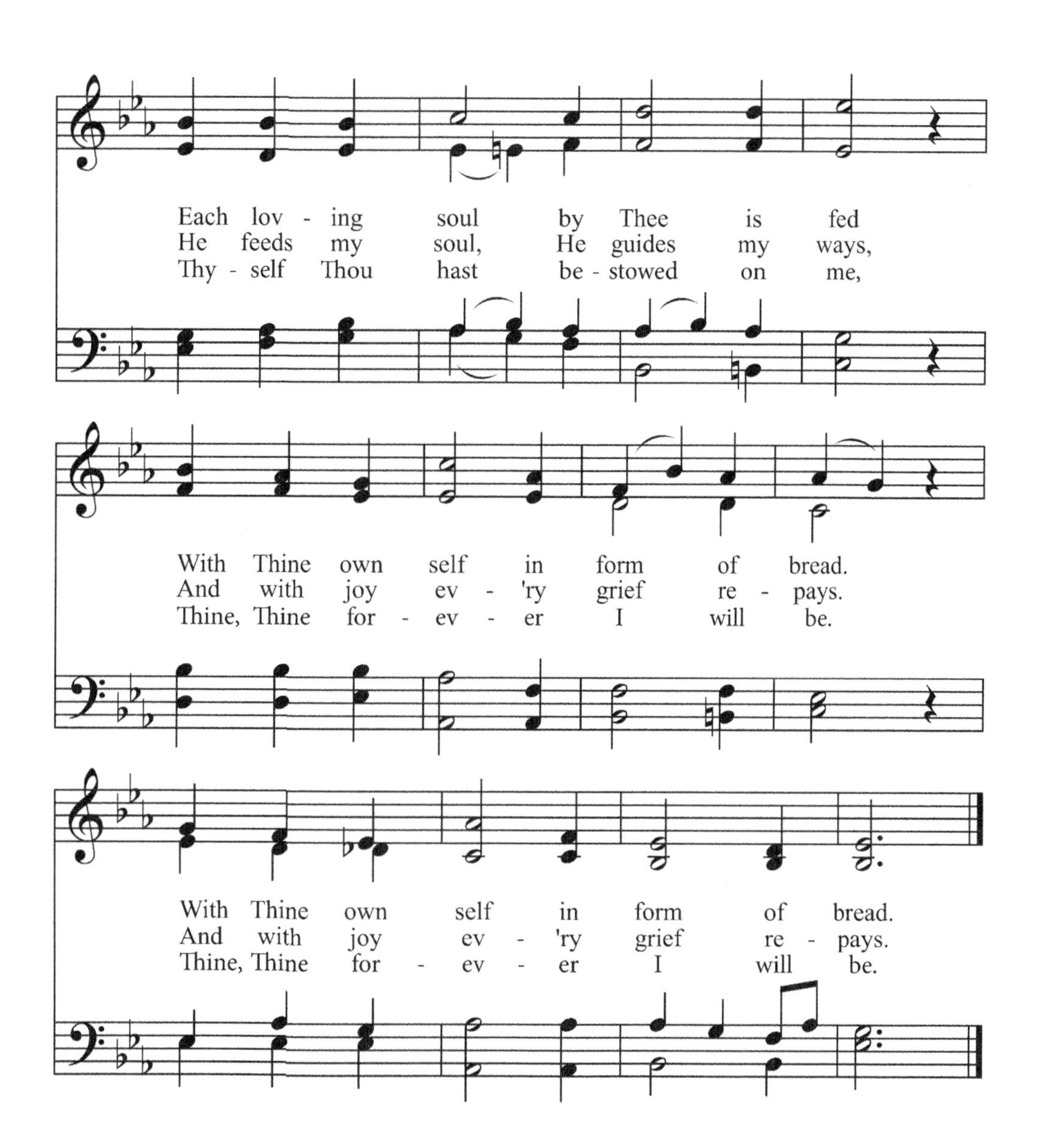
Each lov - ing soul by Thee is fed
He feeds my soul, He guides my ways,
Thy - self Thou hast be - stowed on me,
With Thine own self in form of bread.
And with joy ev - 'ry grief re - pays.
Thine, Thine for - ev - er I will be.
With Thine own self in form of bread.
And with joy ev - 'ry grief re - pays.
Thine, Thine for - ev - er I will be.

O BREAD OF HEAVEN

GILCHRIST 88. 88. 88. 88. G. HERBERT
ST. ALPHONSUS

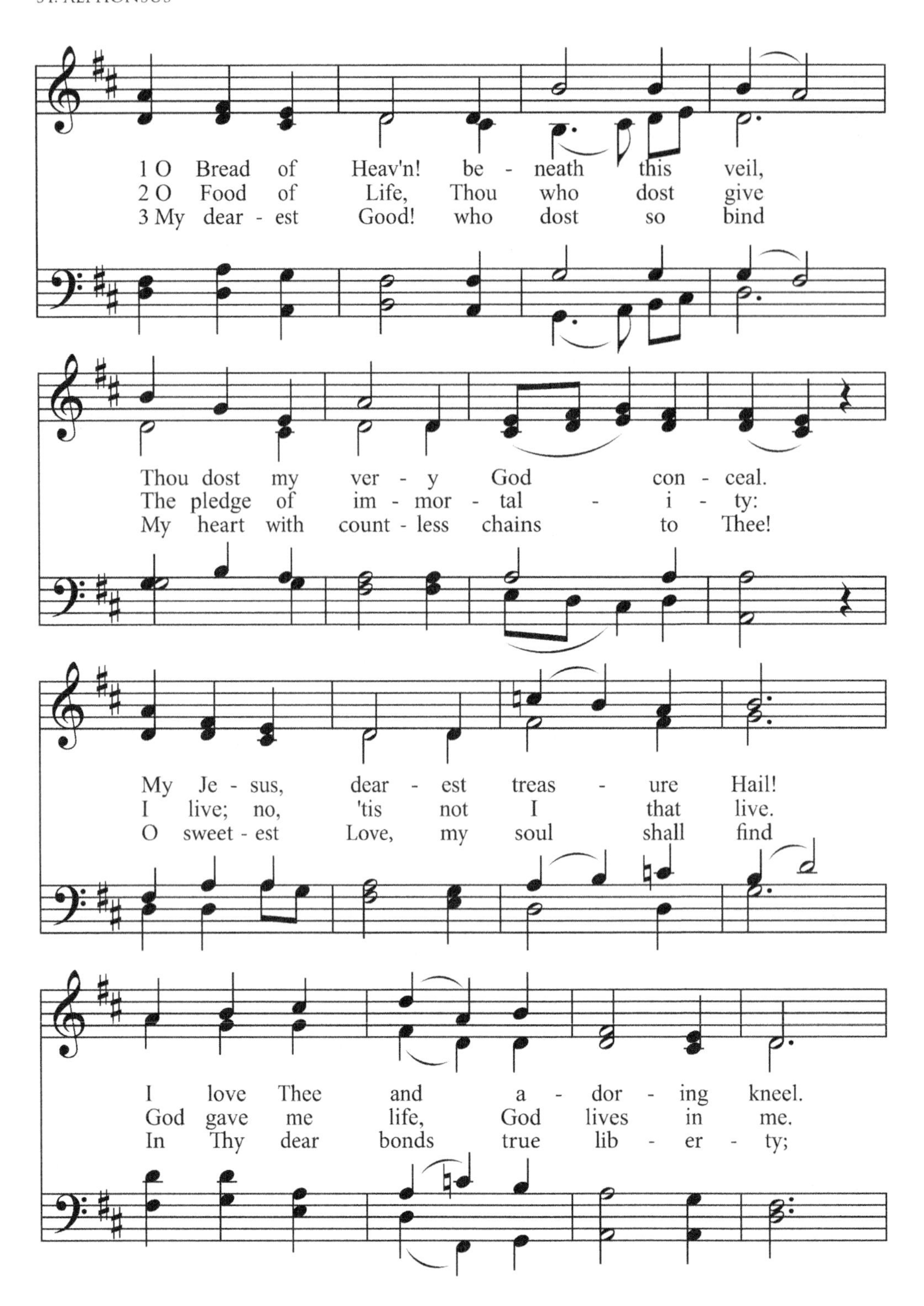

1. O Bread of Heav'n! beneath this veil,
Thou dost my very God conceal.
My Jesus, dearest treasure Hail!
I love Thee and adoring kneel.

2. O Food of Life, Thou who dost give
The pledge of immortality:
I live; no, 'tis not I that live.
God gave me life, God lives in me.

3. My dearest Good! who dost so bind
My heart with countless chains to Thee!
O sweetest Love, my soul shall find
In Thy dear bonds true liberty;

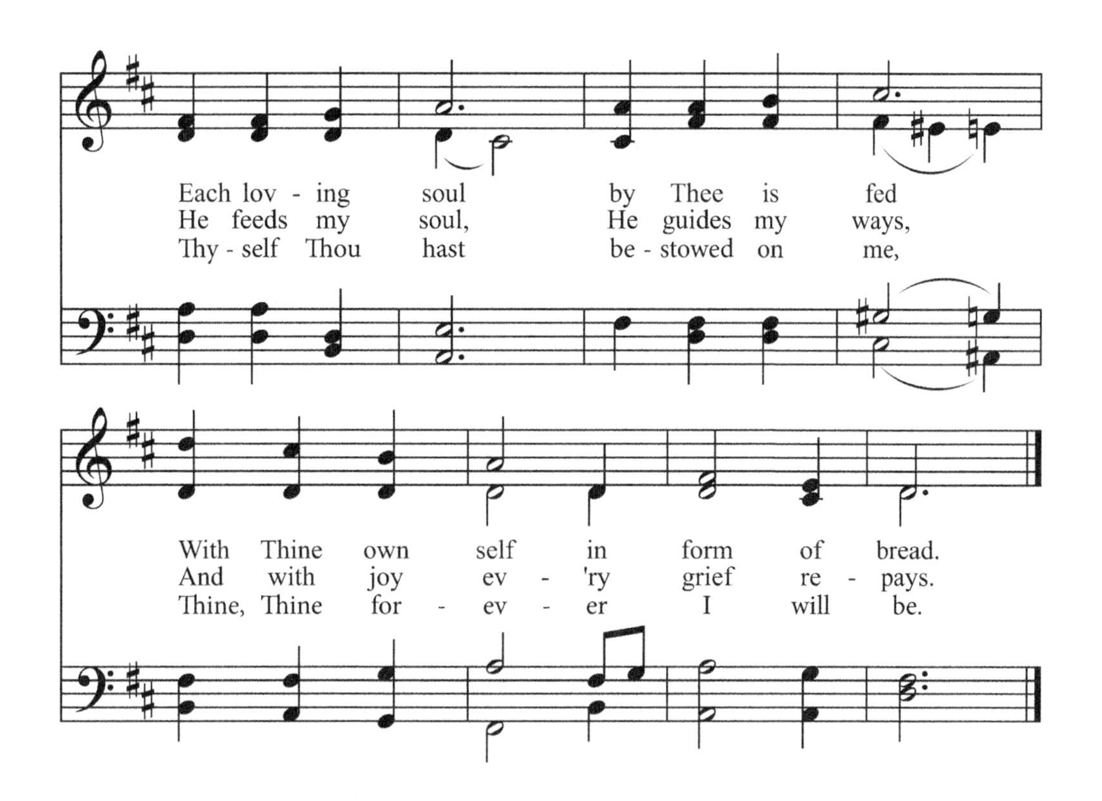
Each lov - ing soul by Thee is fed
He feeds my soul, He guides my ways,
Thy - self Thou hast be - stowed on me,
With Thine own self in form of bread.
And with joy ev - 'ry grief re - pays.
Thine, Thine for - ev - er I will be.

O CHRIST, TO YOU, WE BRING

CONCORD 10. 10. 10. 10. D. ©2009 MARK WINCHESTER
FROM: O CHRIST, YOU PRAYED, MARK WINCHESTER

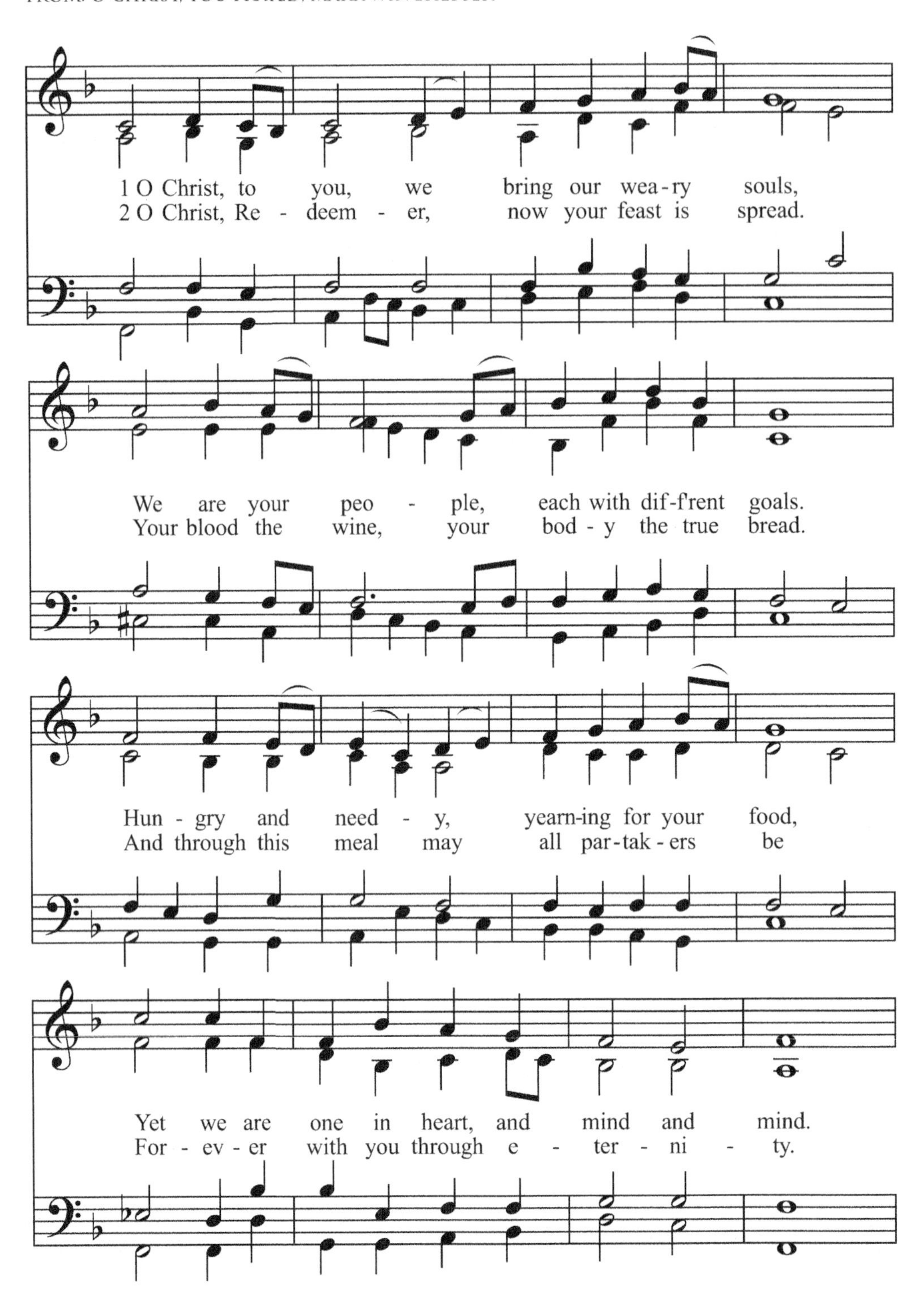

1. O Christ, to you, we bring our weary souls,
We are your people, each with dif-f'rent goals.
Hungry and needy, yearning for your food,
Yet we are one in heart, and mind and mind.

2. O Christ, Redeemer, now your feast is spread.
Your blood the wine, your body the true bread.
And through this meal may all partakers be
Forever with you through eternity.

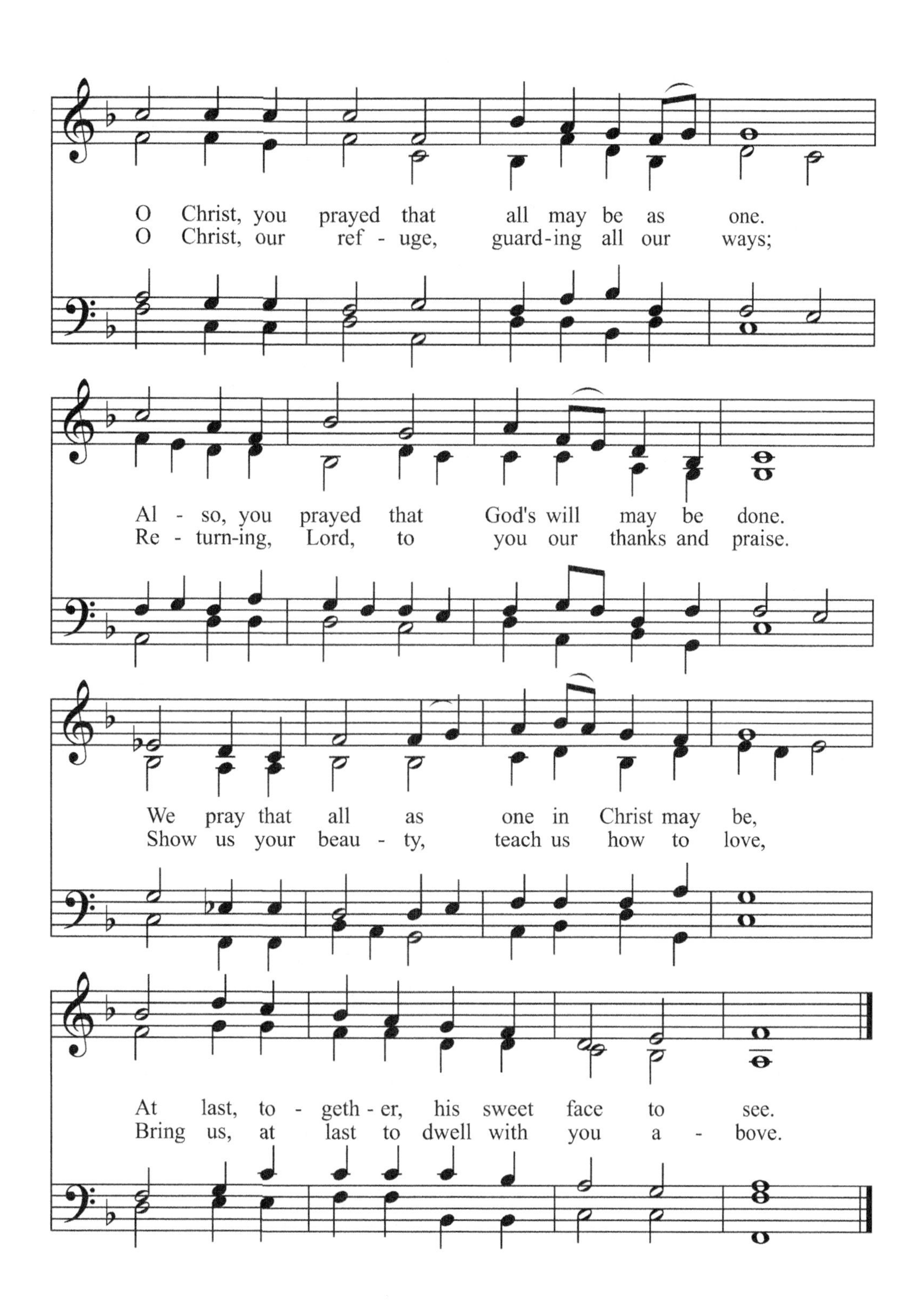
O Christ, you prayed that all may be as one.
O Christ, our ref - uge, guard-ing all our ways;
Al - so, you prayed that God's will may be done.
Re - turn-ing, Lord, to you our thanks and praise.
We pray that all as one in Christ may be,
Show us your beau - ty, teach us how to love,
At last, to - geth - er, his sweet face to see.
Bring us, at last to dwell with you a - bove.

O CHRIST, TO YOU, WE BRING

SONG ONE 10. 10. 10. 10. D. ORLANDO GIBBONS
FROM: O CHRIST, YOU PRAYED, MARK WINCHESTER

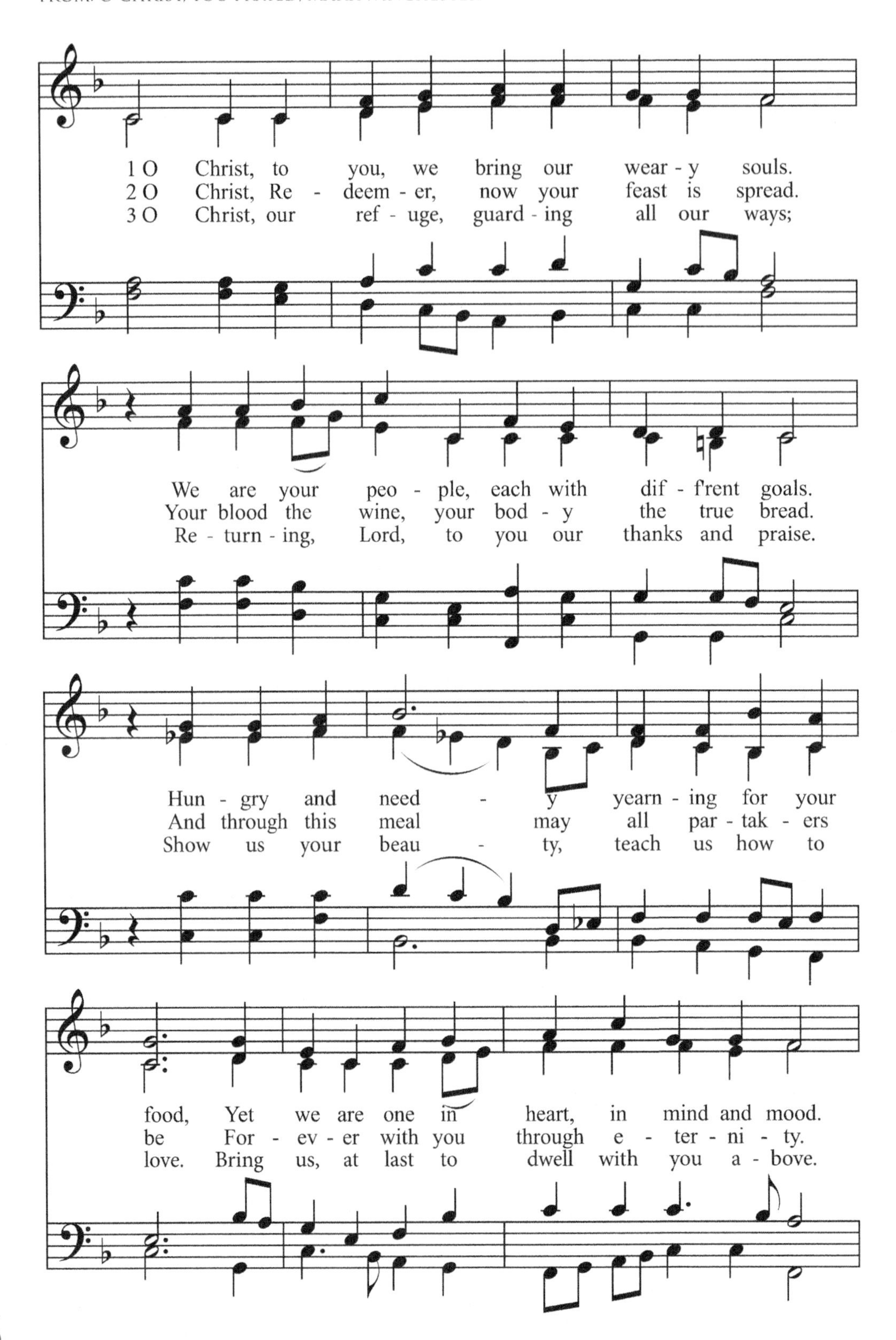

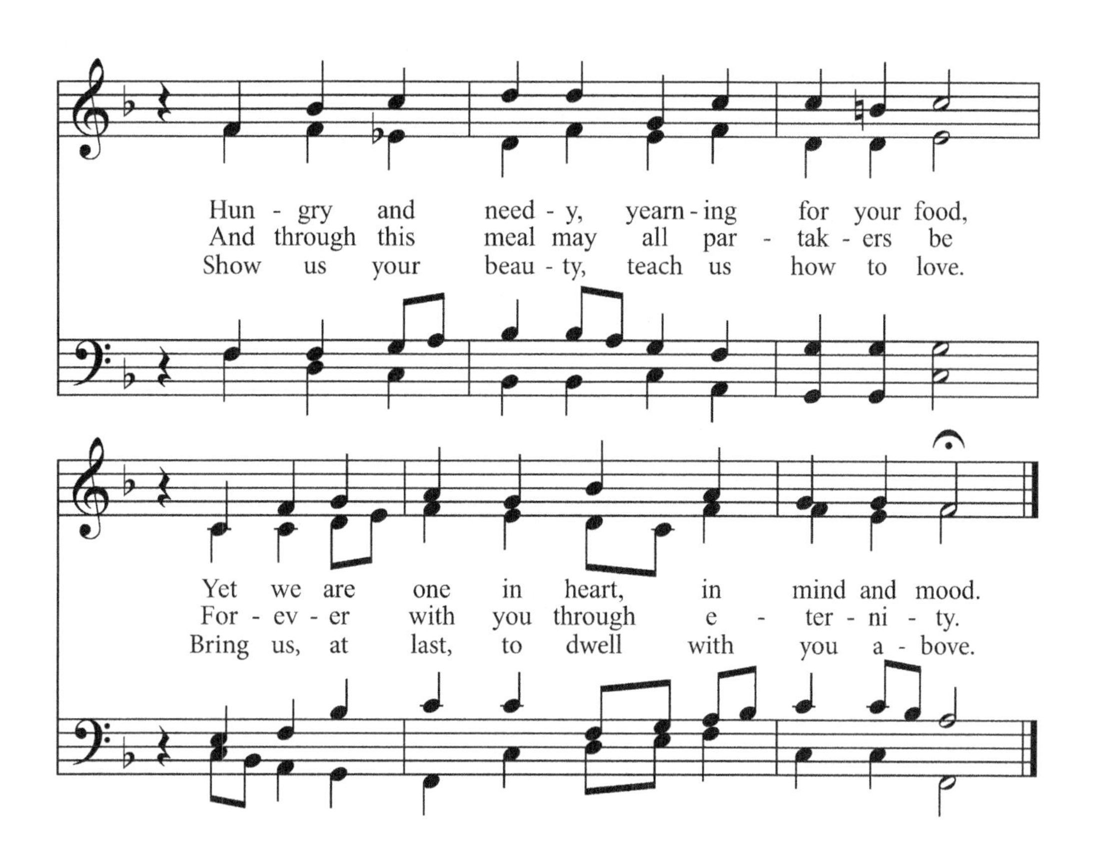
Hun - gry and need - y, yearn - ing for your food,
And through this meal may all par - tak - ers be
Show us your beau - ty, teach us how to love.
Yet we are one in heart, in mind and mood.
For - ev - er with you through e - ter - ni - ty.
Bring us, at last, to dwell with you a - bove.

O FOOD THAT WEARY PILGRIMS LOVE

RADCLIFF 88. 6. 88. 66.

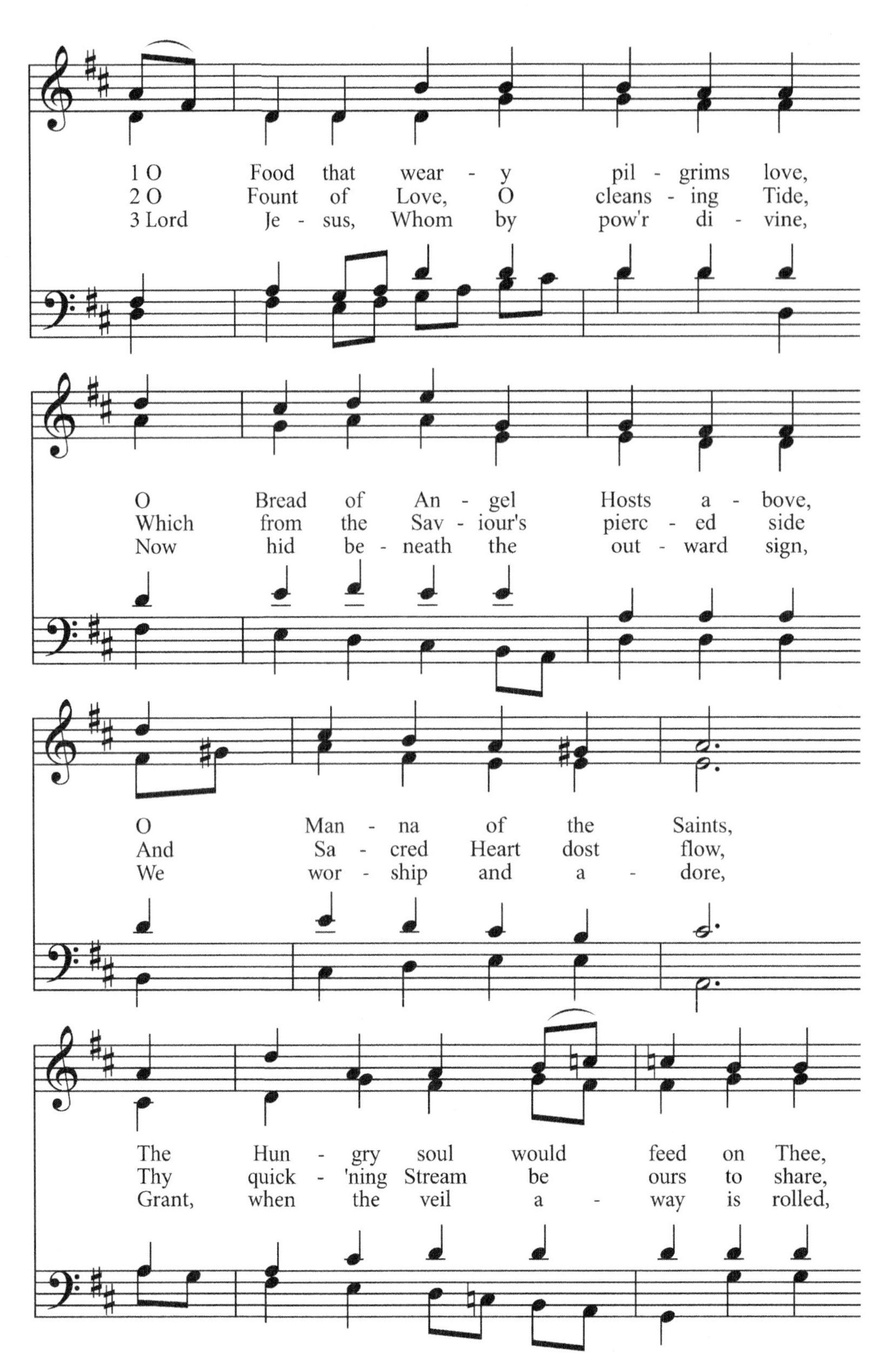

1. O Food that weary pilgrims love, O Bread of Angel Hosts above, O Manna of the Saints, The Hungry soul would feed on Thee,
2. O Fount of Love, O cleansing Tide, Which from the Saviour's pierced side And Sacred Heart dost flow, Thy quick'ning Stream be ours to share,
3. Lord Jesus, Whom by pow'r divine, Now hid beneath the outward sign, We worship and adore, Grant, when the veil away is rolled,

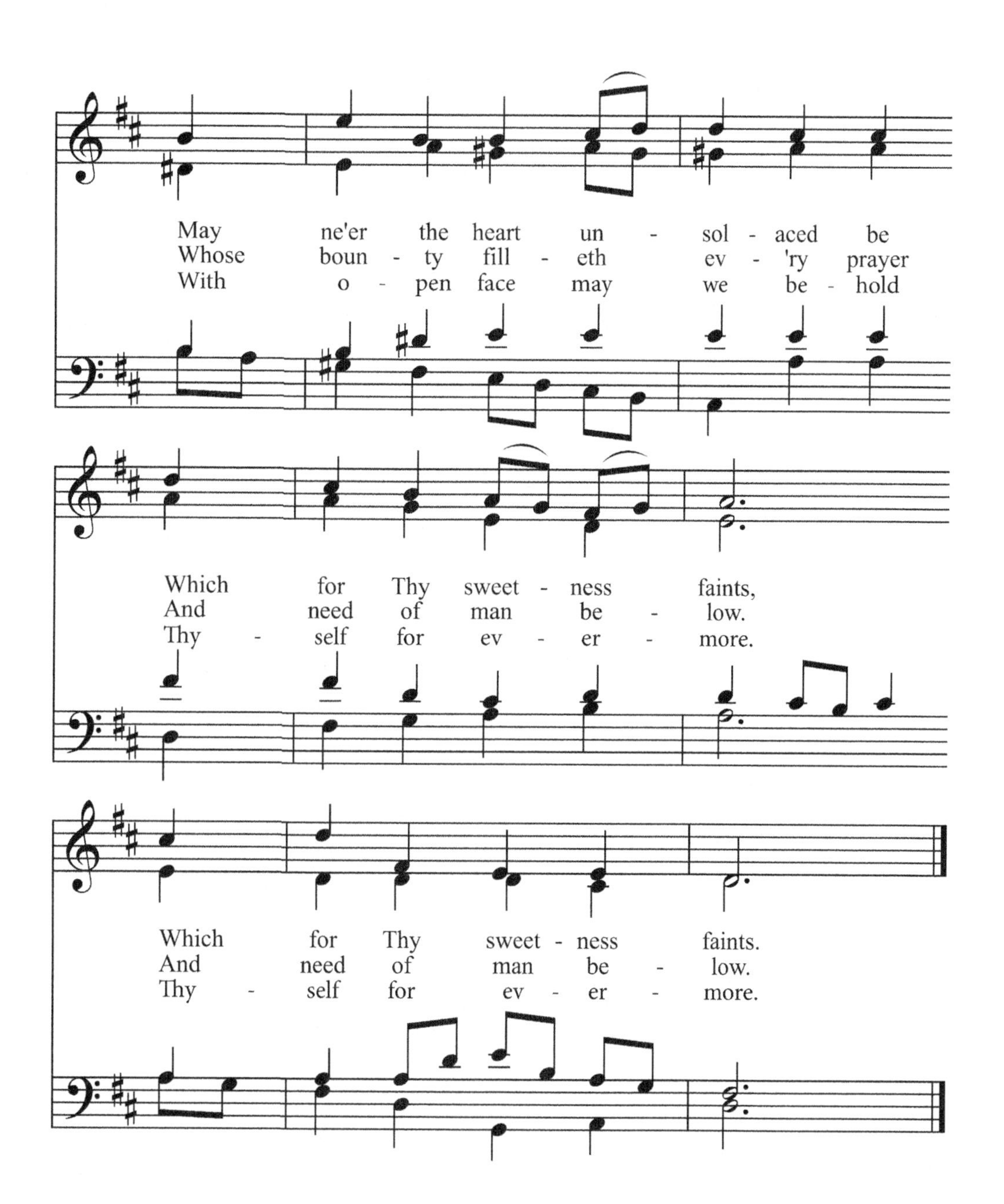
May ne'er the heart un - sol - aced be
Whose boun - ty fill - eth ev - 'ry prayer
With o - pen face may we be - hold
Which for Thy sweet - ness faints,
And need of man be - low.
Thy - self for ev - er - more.
Which for Thy sweet - ness faints.
And need of man be - low.
Thy - self for ev - er - more.

O FOOD, THE PILGRIM NEEDETH

ABBOT 776. 776. D.
O ESCA VIATORUM

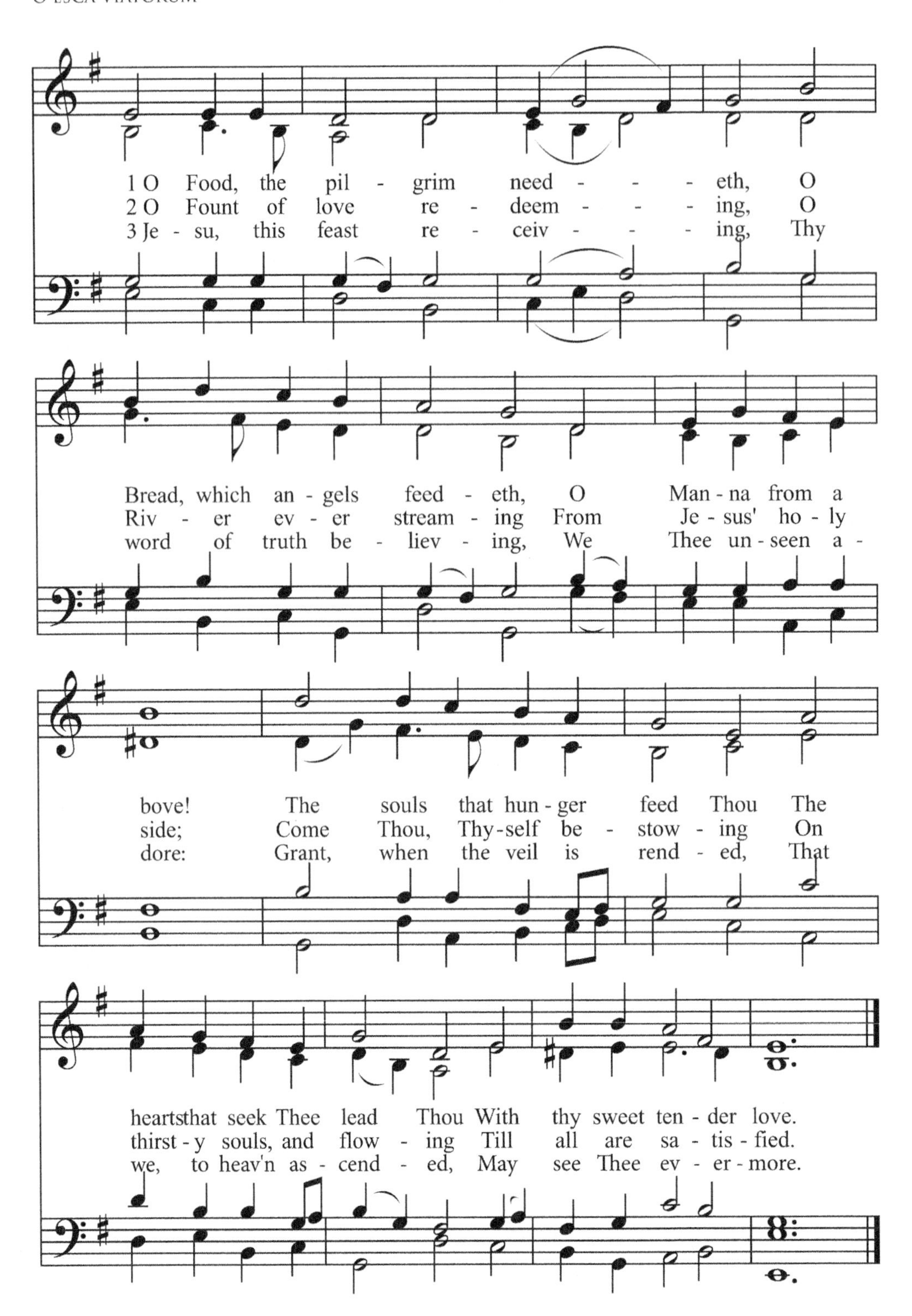

1. O Food, the pilgrim needeth, O Bread, which angels feedeth, O Manna from above! The souls that hunger feed Thou The hearts that seek Thee lead Thou With thy sweet tender love.

2. O Fount of love redeeming, O River ever streaming From Jesus' holy side; Come Thou, Thyself bestowing On thirsty souls, and flowing Till all are satisfied.

3. Jesu, this feast receiving, Thy word of truth believing, We Thee unseen adore: Grant, when the veil is rended, That we, to heav'n ascended, May see Thee evermore.

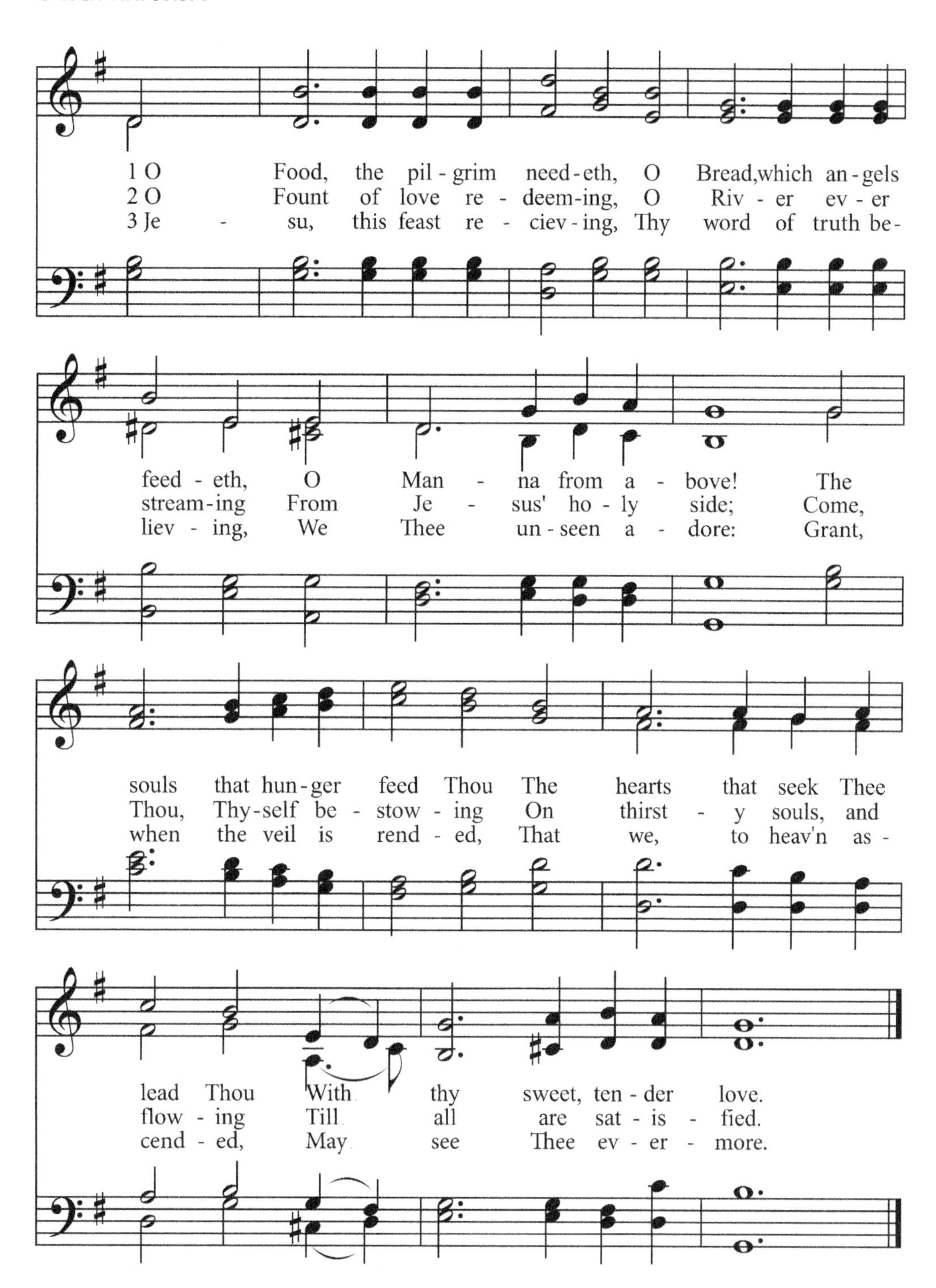

O GOD UNSEEN, YET EVER NEAR

THIRD MODE MELODY C. M. D. THOMAS TALLIS
EDWARD OSLER

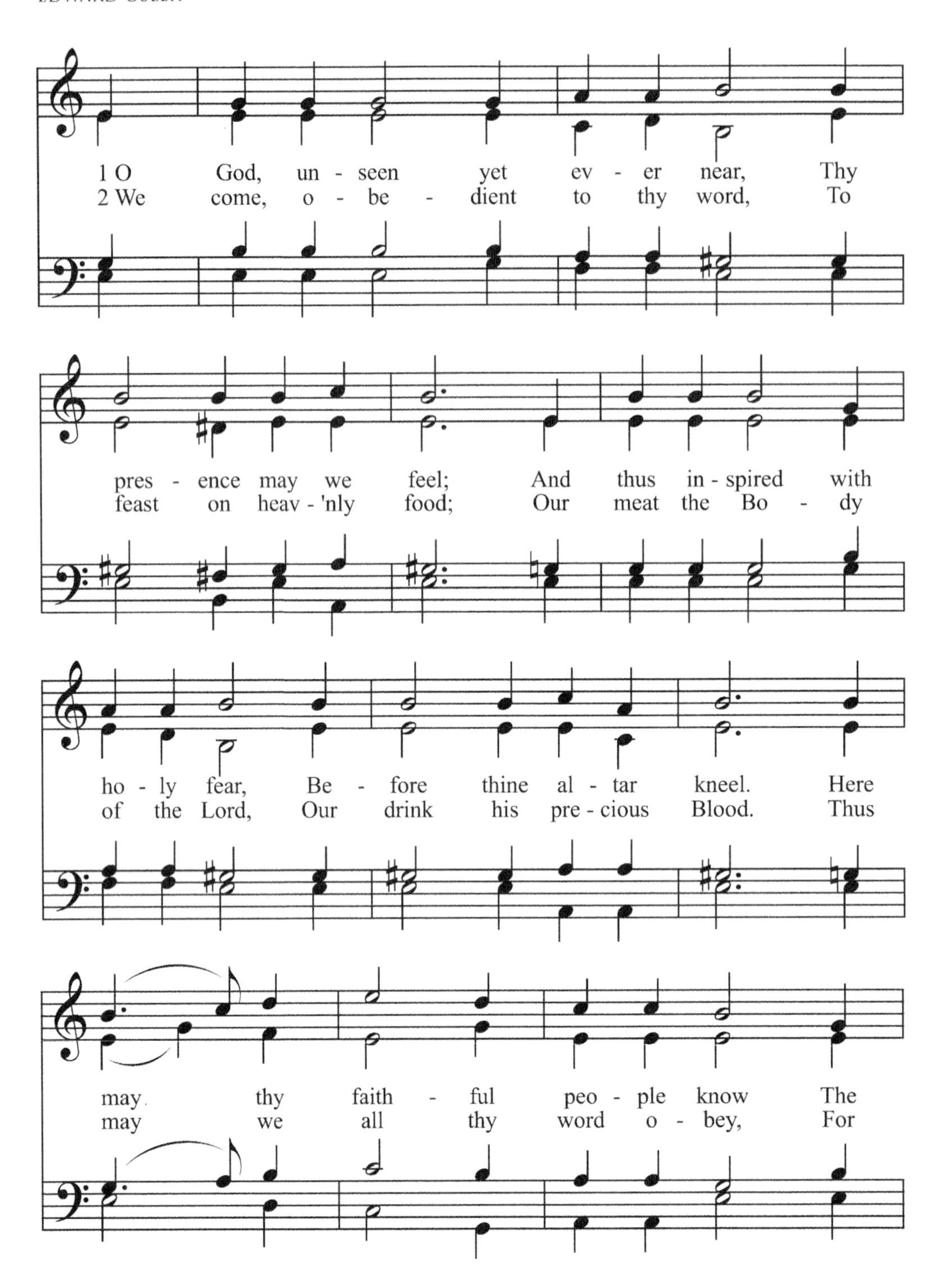

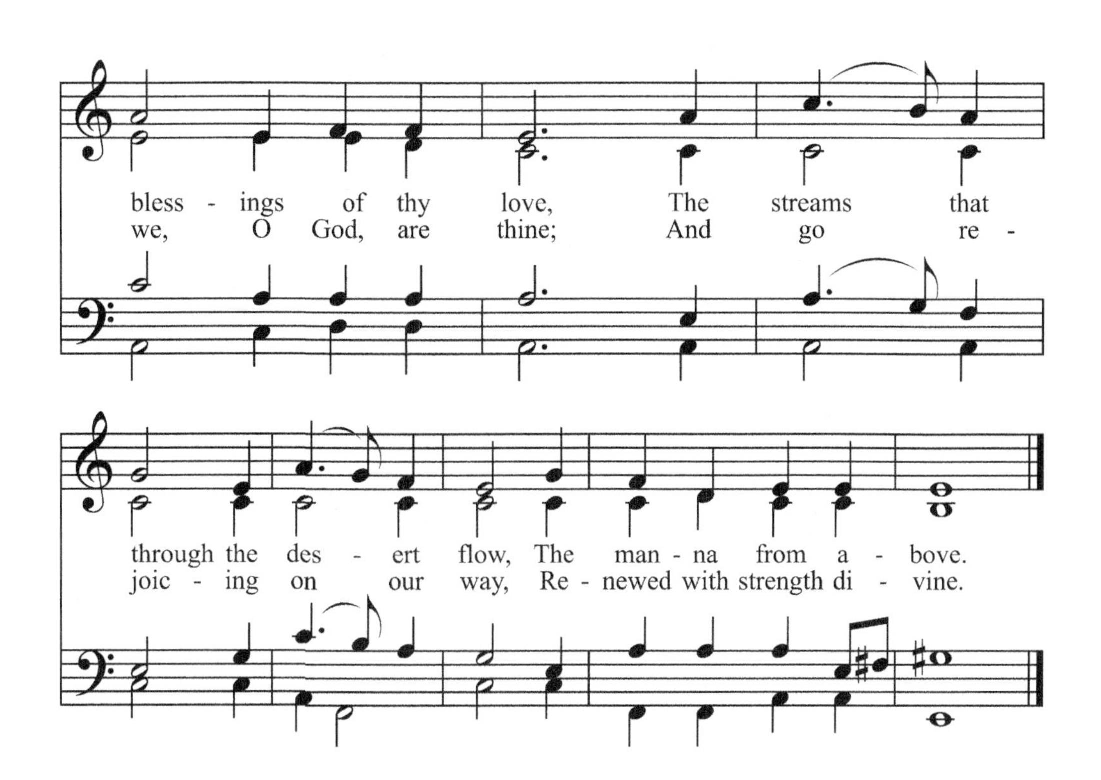

bless - ings of thy love, The streams that
we, O God, are thine; And go re -
through the des - ert flow, The man - na from a - bove.
joic - ing on our way, Re - newed with strength di - vine.

O GODHEAD HID

CHAMBERLAIN 11. 11. 10. 10. RICHARD TERRY
TR. REV. EDWARD CASWELL

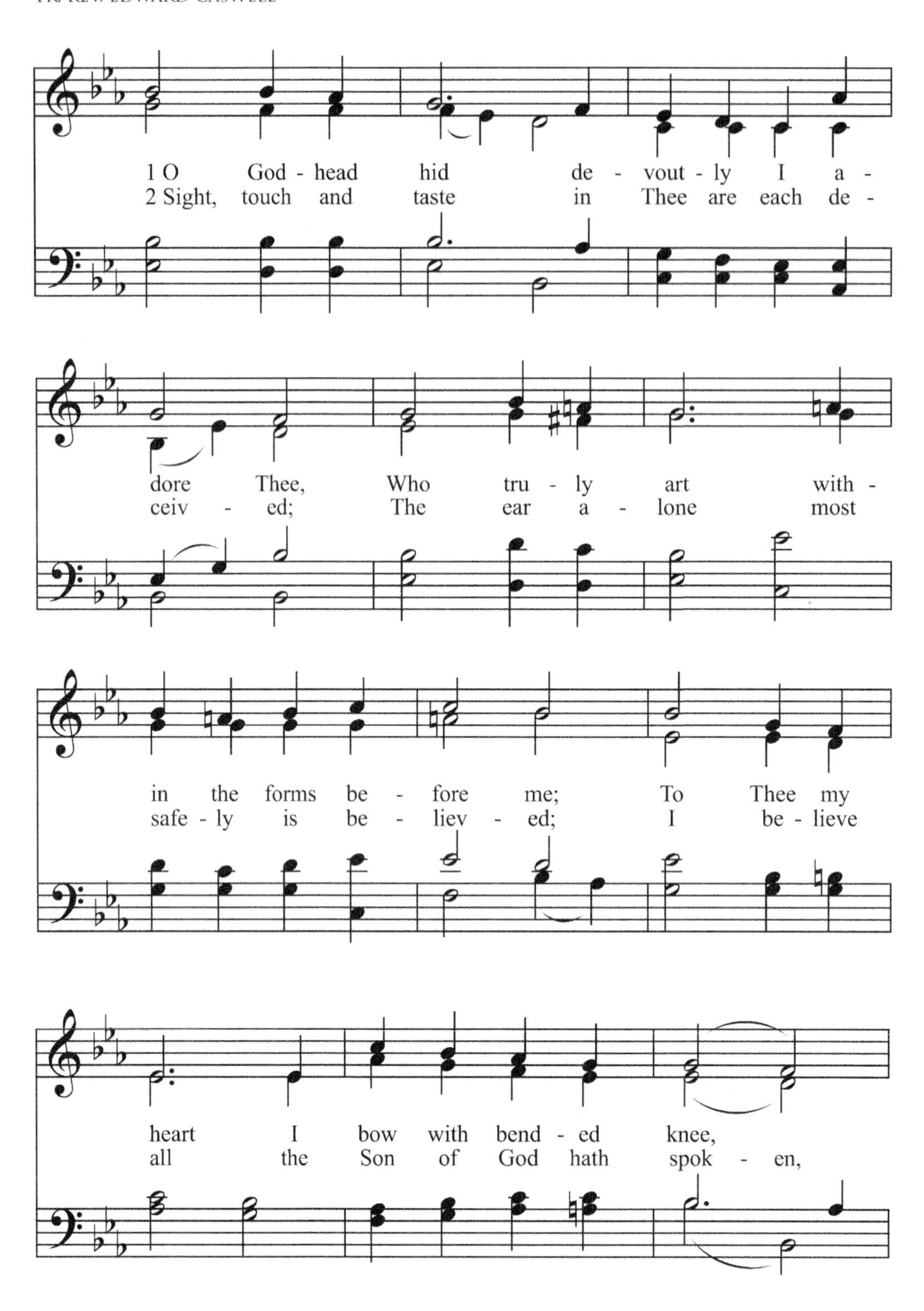

1 O God-head hid devoutly I adore Thee, Who truly art within the forms before me; To Thee my heart I bow with bended knee,

2 Sight, touch and taste in Thee are each deceived; The ear alone most safely is believed; I believe all the Son of God hath spoken,

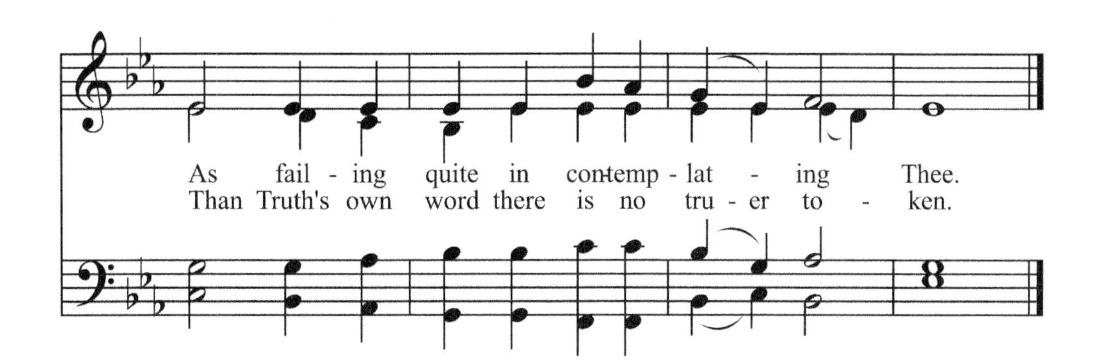
As fail - ing quite in contemp - lat - ing Thee.
Than Truth's own word there is no tru - er to - ken.

O JESUS CHRIST, REDEEMER

KIRKWOOD 76. 76. D.

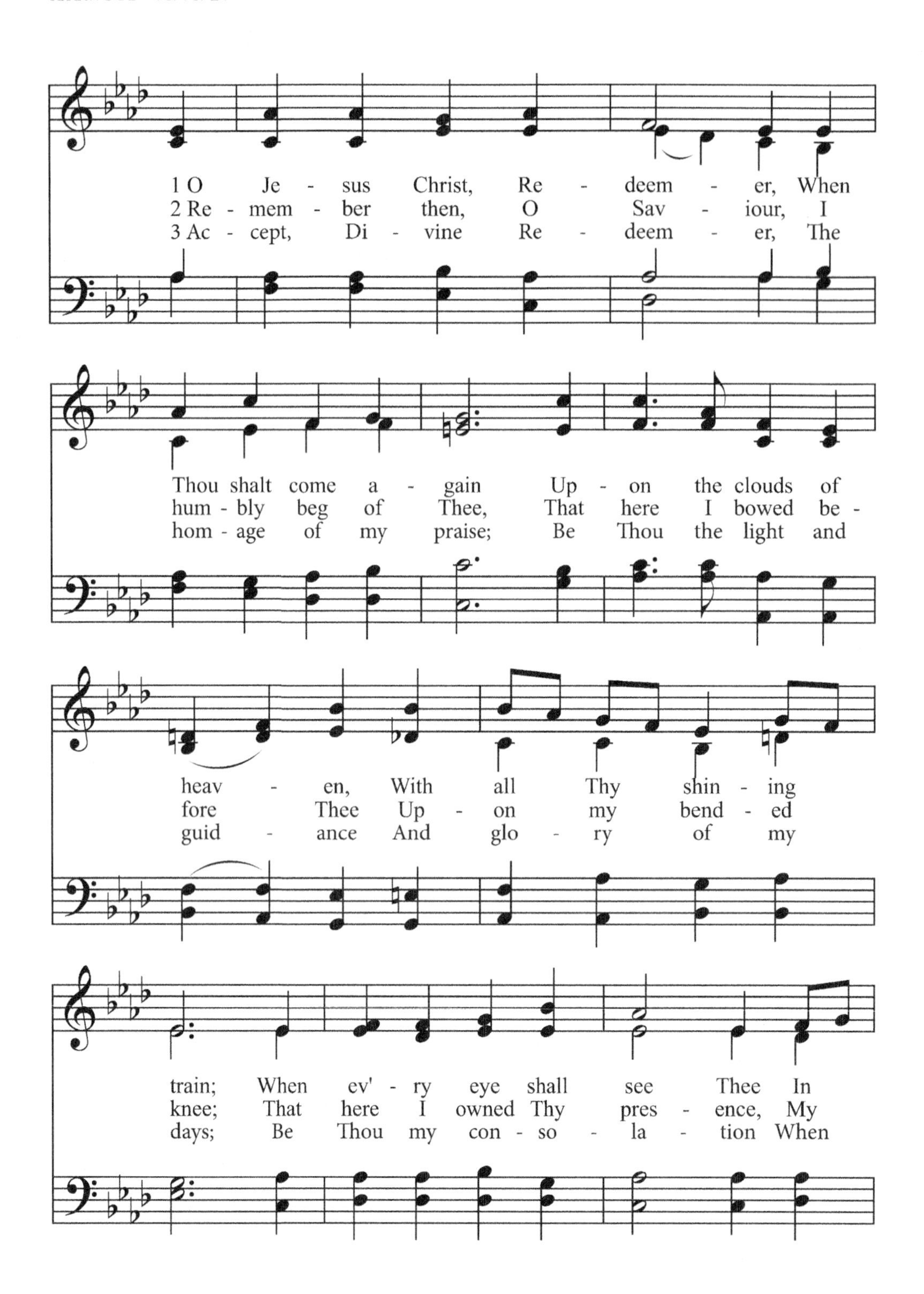

1. O Jesus Christ, Redeemer, When Thou shalt come again Upon the clouds of heaven, With all Thy shining train; When ev'ry eye shall see Thee In
2. Remember then, O Saviour, I humbly beg of Thee, That here I bowed before Thee Upon my bended knee; That here I owned Thy presence, My
3. Accept, Divine Redeemer, The homage of my praise; Be Thou the light and guidance And glory of my days; Be Thou my consolation When

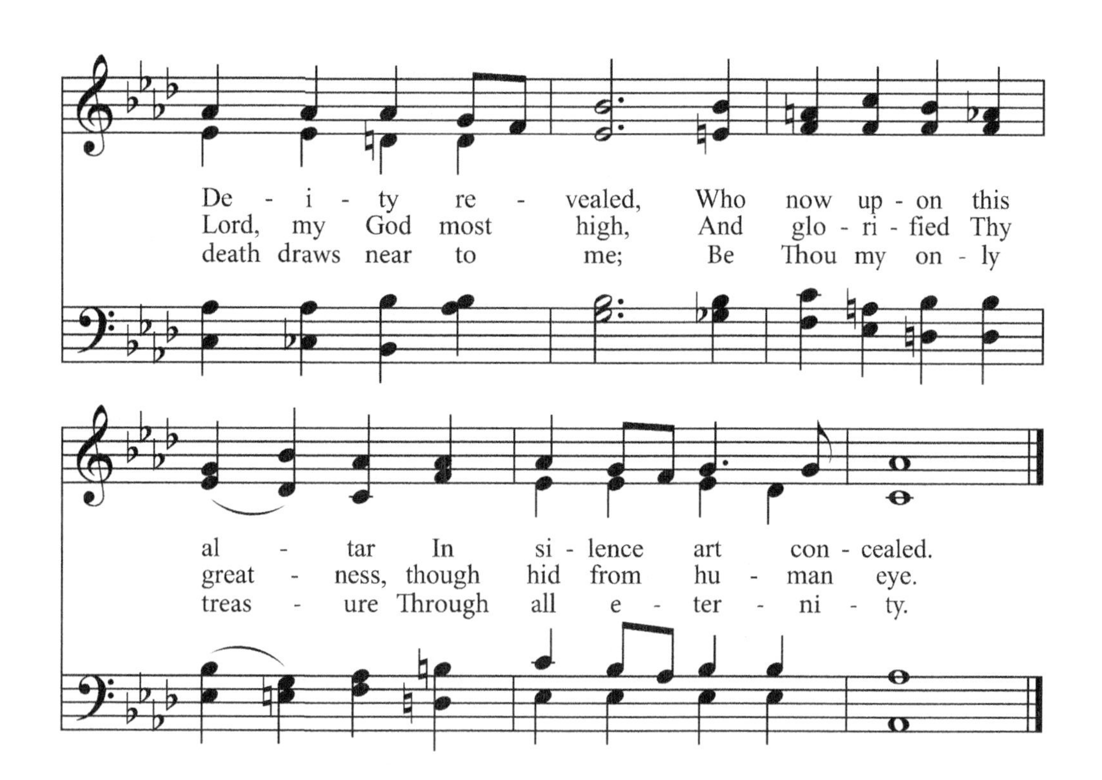
De - i - ty re - vealed, Who now up - on this
Lord, my God most high, And glo - ri - fied Thy
death draws near to me; Be Thou my on - ly
al - tar In si - lence art con - cealed.
great - ness, though hid from hu - man eye.
treas - ure Through all e - ter - ni - ty.

O JESUS CHRIST, REDEEMER

KENTWORTH 76. 76. D.

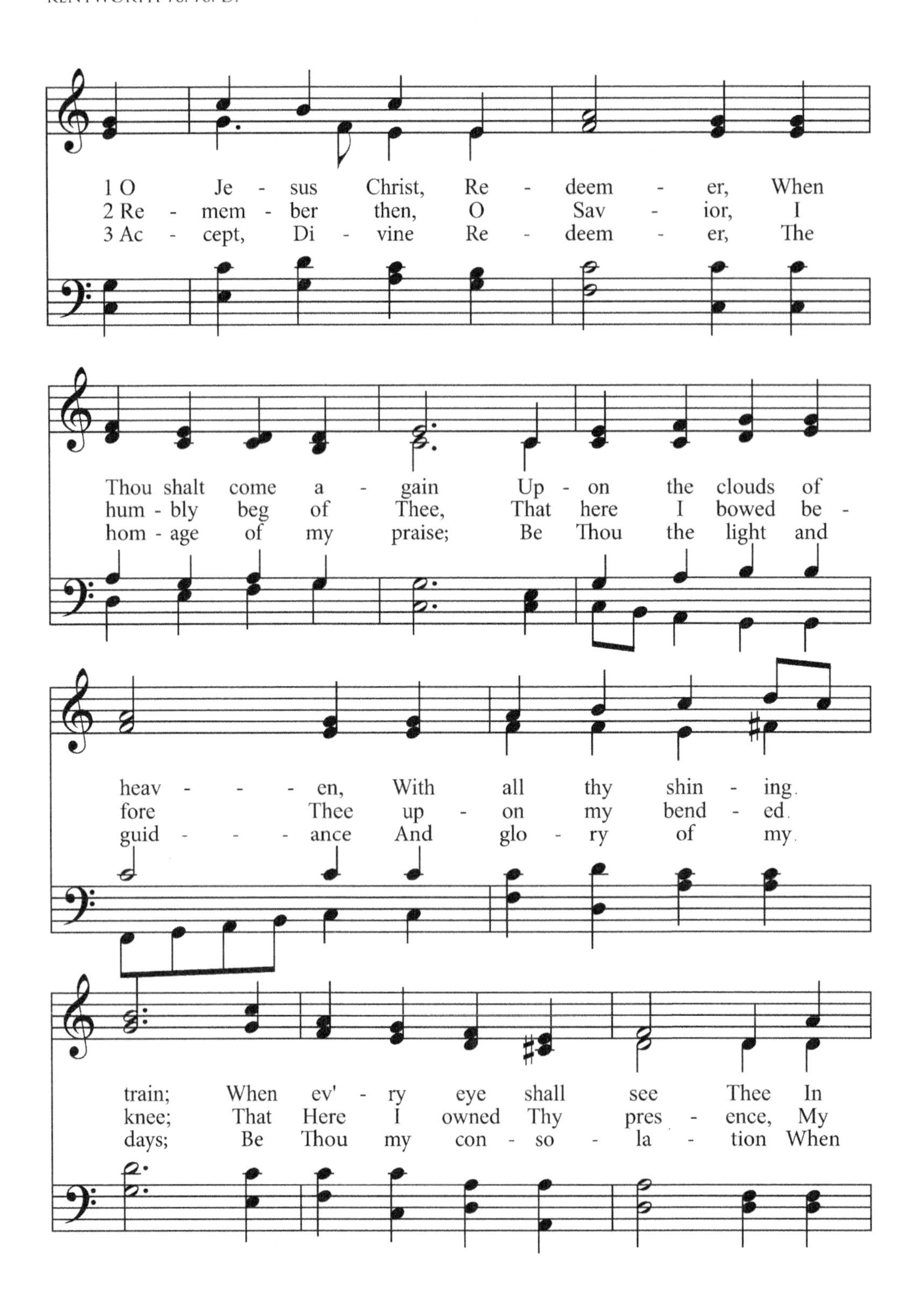

1. O Jesus Christ, Redeemer, When Thou shalt come again Upon the clouds of heaven, With all thy shining train; When ev'ry eye shall see Thee In
2. Remember then, O Savior, I humbly beg of Thee, That here I bowed before Thee upon my bended knee; That Here I owned Thy presence, My
3. Accept, Divine Redeemer, The homage of my praise; Be Thou the light and guidance And glory of my days; Be Thou my consolation When

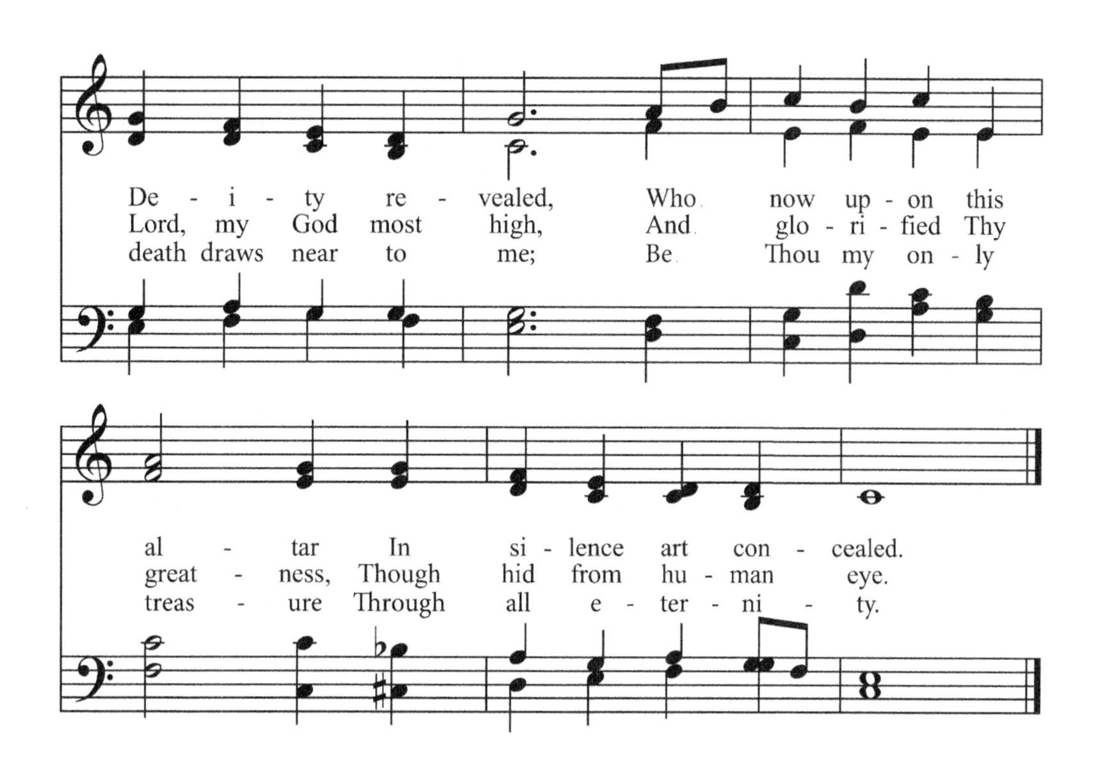
De - i - ty re - vealed, Who now up - on this
Lord, my God most high, And glo - ri - fied Thy
death draws near to me; Be Thou my on - ly
al - tar In si - lence art con - cealed.
great - ness, Though hid from hu - man eye.
treas - ure Through all e - ter - ni - ty.

O JESUS, THOU THE GLORY ART

DULCET 86. 86.

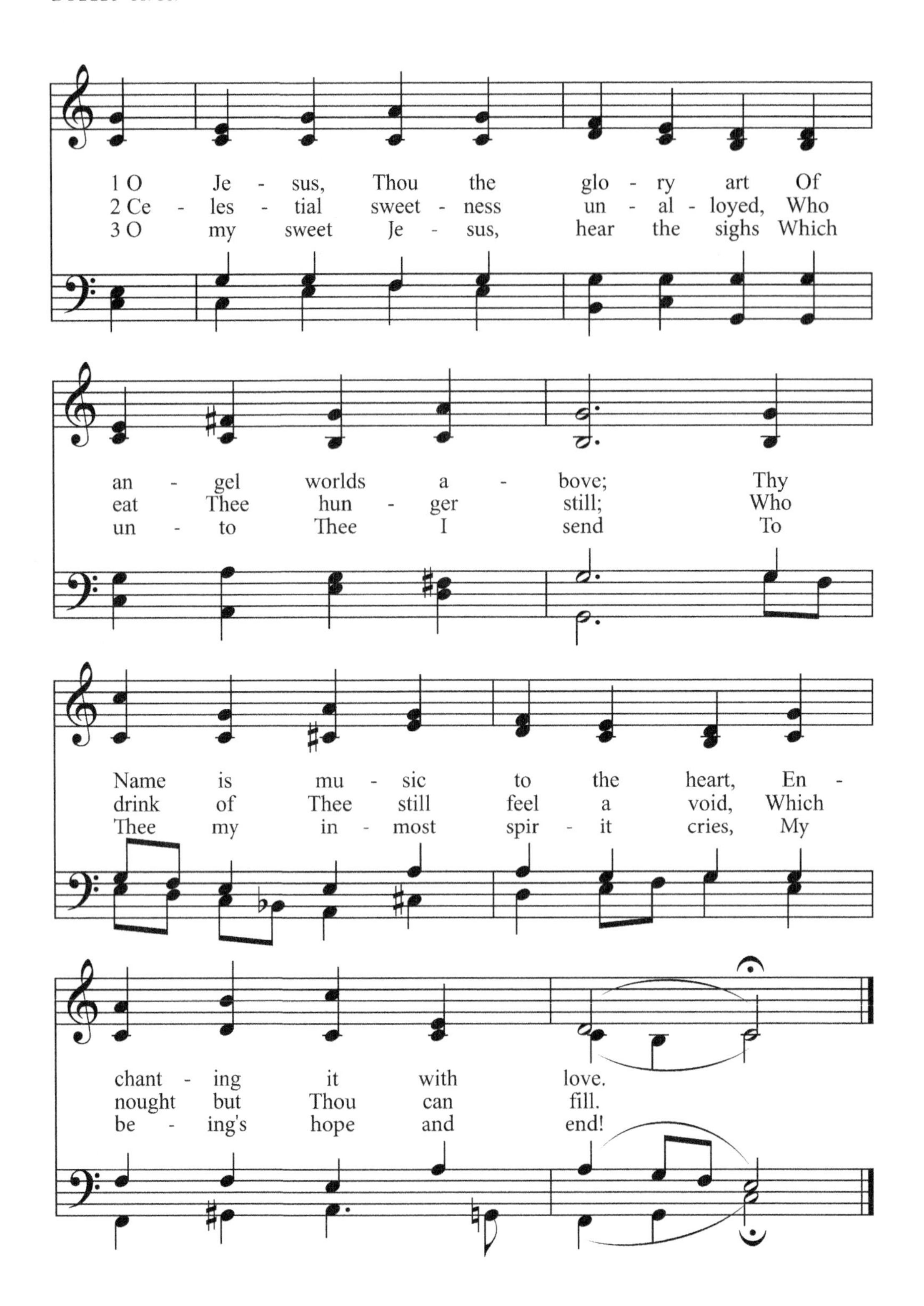

1. O Jesus, Thou the glory art Of angel worlds above; Thy Name is music to the heart, Enchanting it with love.
2. Celestial sweetness unalloyed, Who eat Thee hunger still; Who drink of Thee still feel a void, Which nought but Thou can fill.
3. O my sweet Jesus, hear the sighs Which unto Thee I send; To Thee my inmost spirit cries, My being's hope and end!

O JESUS, LORD, MOST MIGHTY KING

ST. BERNARD 86. 86. S. WEBBE, JR.
TR. J.D. AYLWARD, O.P..

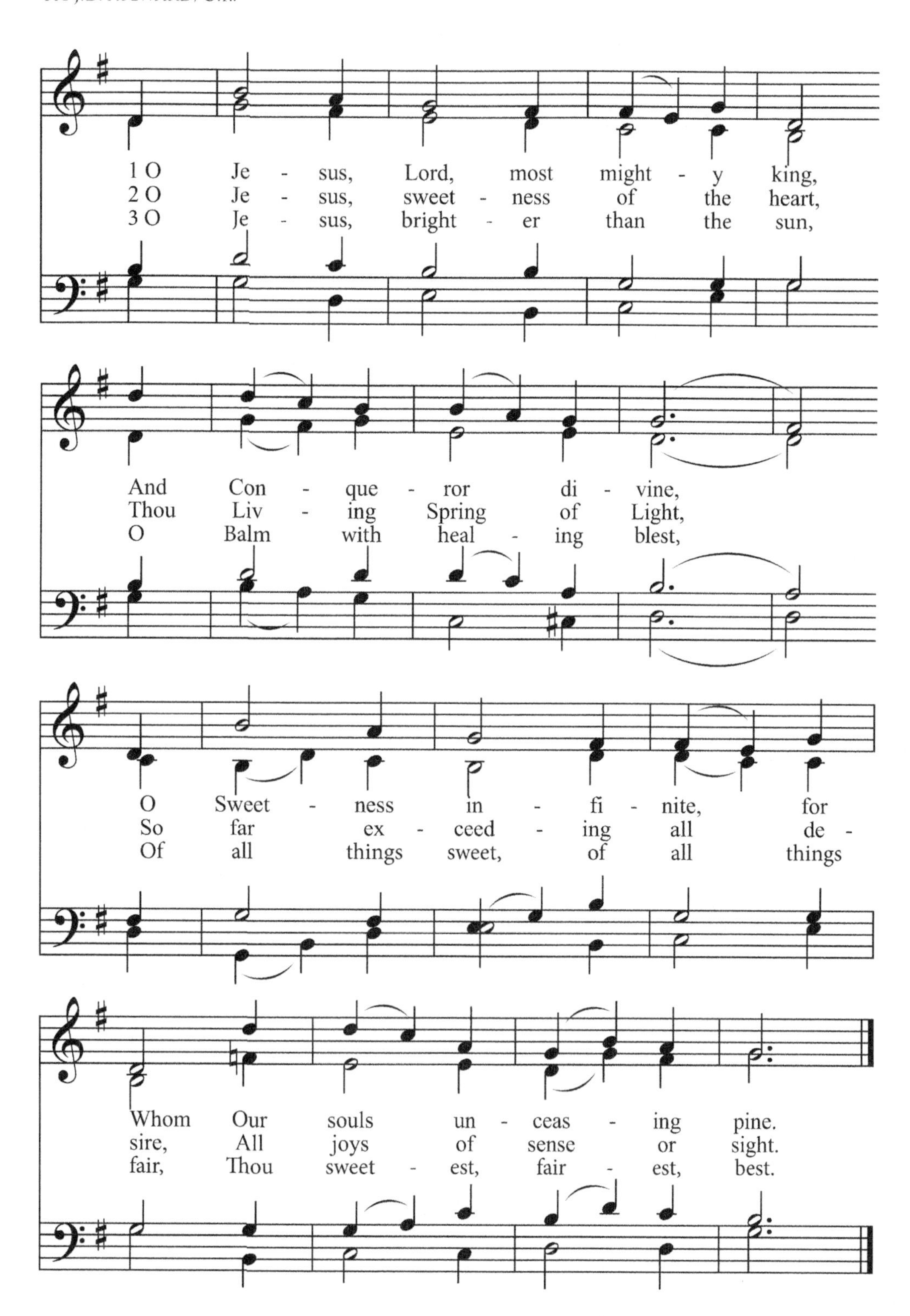

1. O Jesus, Lord, most mighty king,
And Conqueror divine,
O Sweetness infinite, for Whom
Our souls unceasing pine.

2. O Jesus, sweetness of the heart,
Thou Living Spring of Light,
So far exceeding all desire,
All joys of sense or sight.

3. O Jesus, brighter than the sun,
O Balm with healing blest,
Of all things sweet, of all things fair,
Thou sweetest, fairest, best.

O JESUS, LORD, REMEMBER

ORTHODOX CHANT 76. 76. 76. 76.   J.C.S. HARM ©2009 MARK WINCHESTER
REV. EDWARD CASWELL

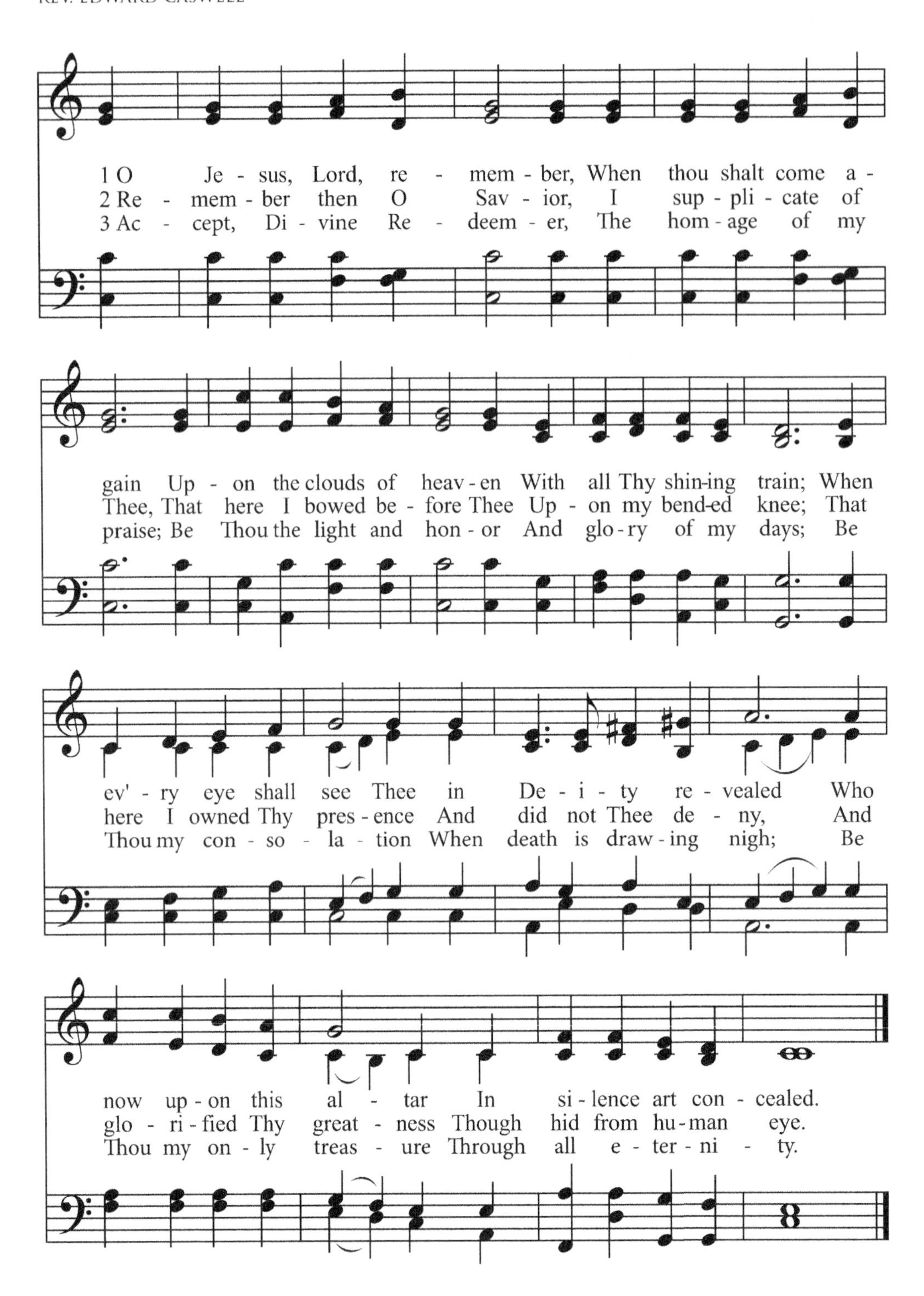

1. O Jesus, Lord, remember, When thou shalt come again Upon the clouds of heaven With all Thy shining train; When ev'ry eye shall see Thee in Deity revealed Who now upon this altar In silence art concealed.

2. Remember then O Savior, I supplicate of Thee, That here I bowed before Thee Upon my bended knee; That here I owned Thy presence And did not Thee deny, And glorified Thy greatness Though hid from human eye.

3. Accept, Divine Redeemer, The homage of my praise; Be Thou the light and honor And glory of my days; Be Thou my consolation When death is drawing nigh; Be Thou my only treasure Through all eternity.

O LORD, I AM NOT WORTHY

FINCH 76. 76.

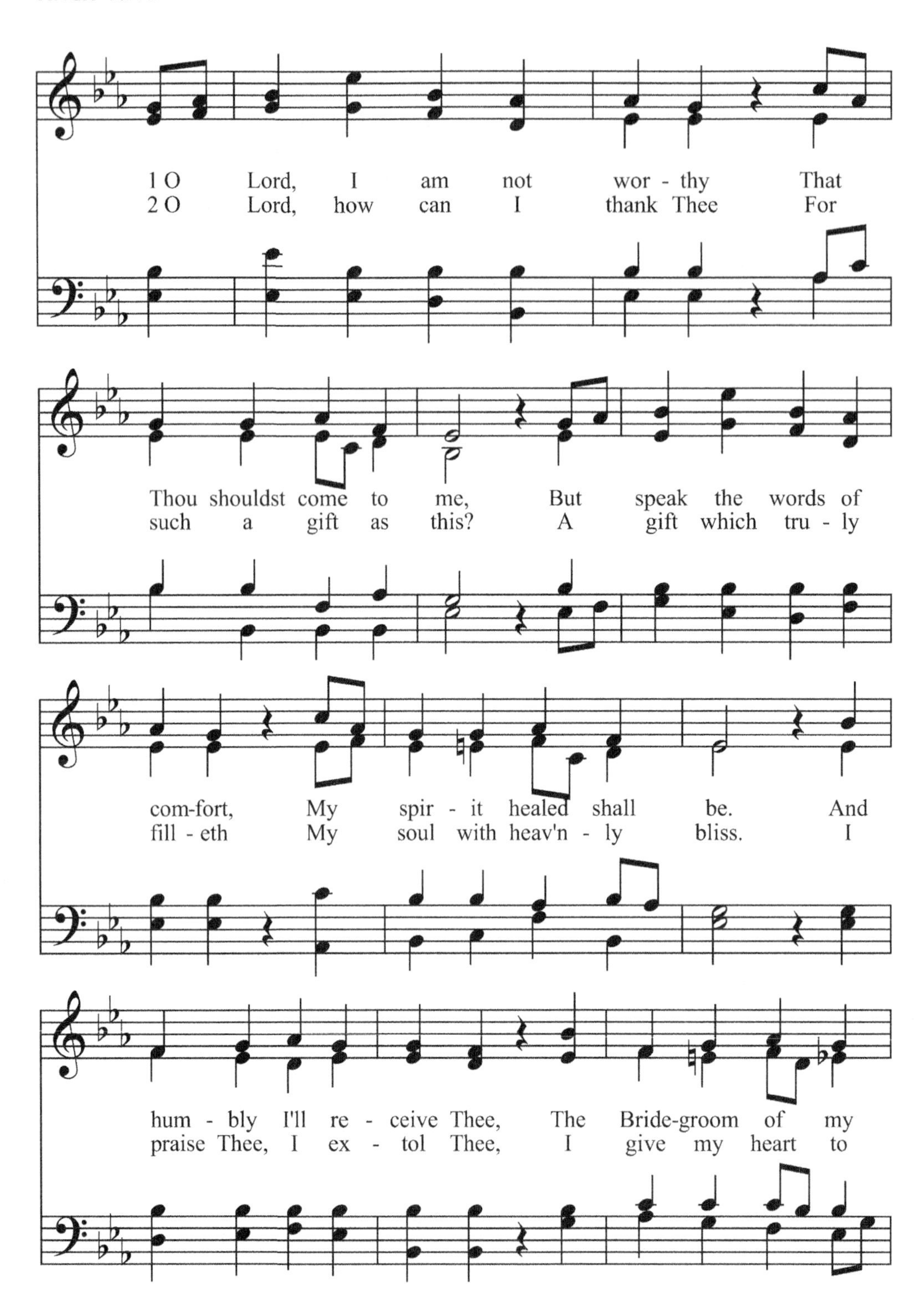

1. O Lord, I am not worthy That Thou shouldst come to me, But speak the words of comfort, My spirit healed shall be. And humbly I'll receive Thee, The Bride-groom of my

2. O Lord, how can I thank Thee For such a gift as this? A gift which truly filleth My soul with heav'nly bliss. I praise Thee, I extol Thee, I give my heart to

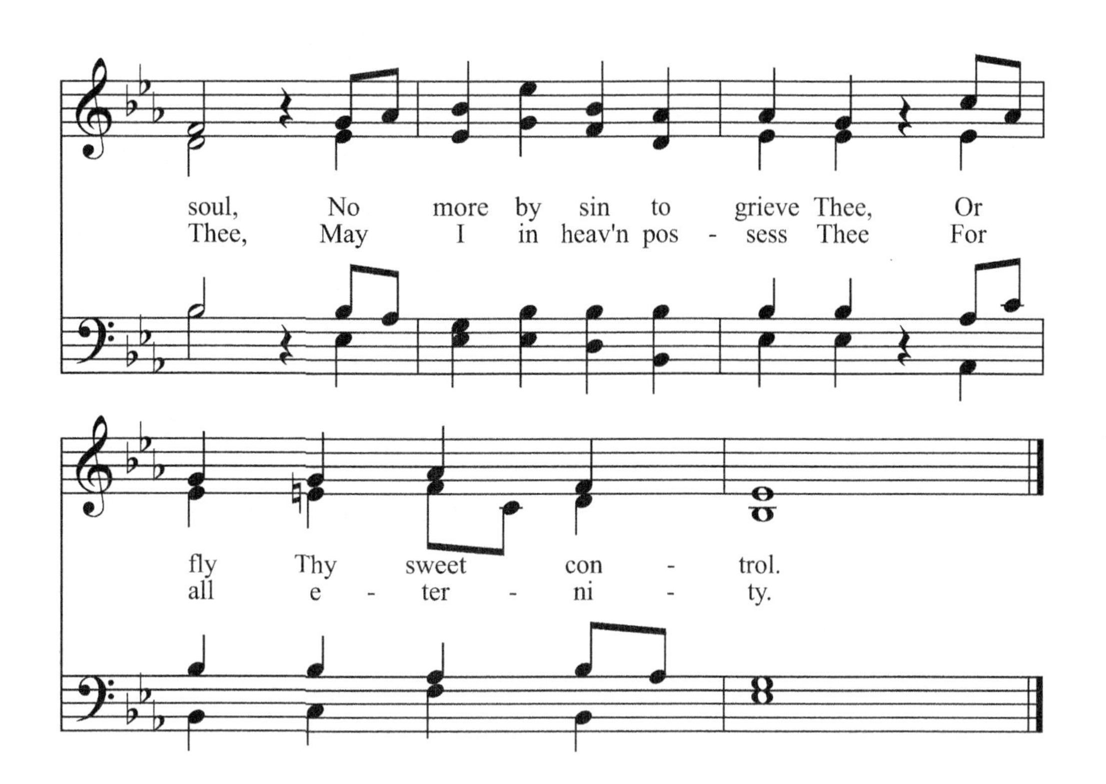
soul, No more by sin to grieve Thee, Or
Thee, May I in heav'n pos - sess Thee For
fly Thy sweet con - trol.
all e - ter - ni - ty.

O LORD, I AM NOT WORTHY

HARLAN 76. 76.

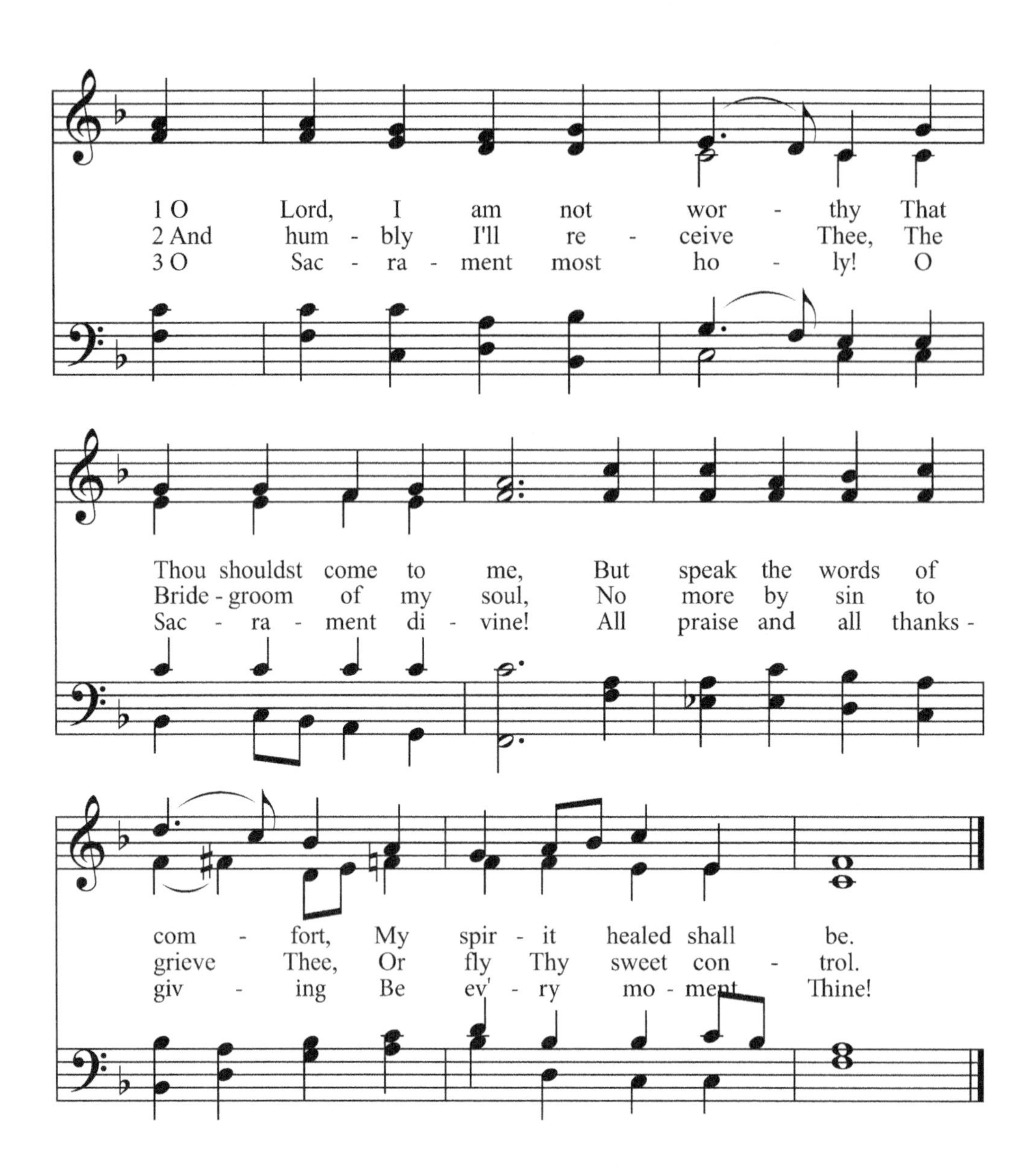

1. O Lord, I am not worthy That Thou shouldst come to me, But speak the words of comfort, My spirit healed shall be.

2. And humbly I'll receive Thee, The Bridegroom of my soul, No more by sin to grieve Thee, Or fly Thy sweet control.

3. O Sacrament most holy! O Sacrament divine! All praise and all thanksgiving Be ev'ry moment Thine!

O LORD, I AM NOT WORTHY

NON DIGNUS 76. 76.

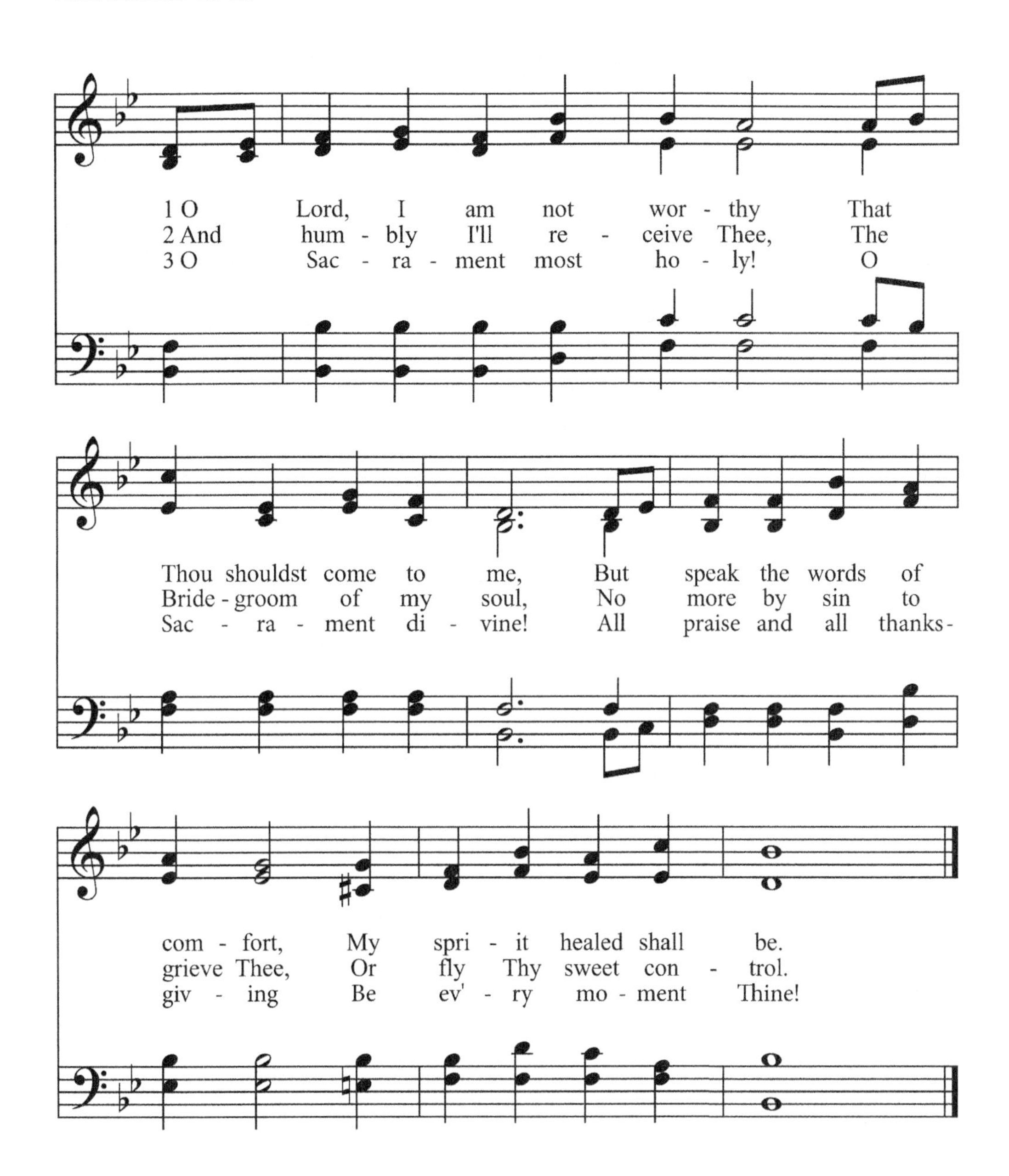

1. O Lord, I am not worthy That Thou shouldst come to me, But speak the words of comfort, My spirit healed shall be.

2. And humbly I'll receive Thee, The Bridegroom of my soul, No more by sin to grieve Thee, Or fly Thy sweet control.

3. O Sacrament most holy! O Sacrament divine! All praise and all thanksgiving Be ev'ry moment Thine!

O SACRAMENT MOST HOLY

TRADITIONAL

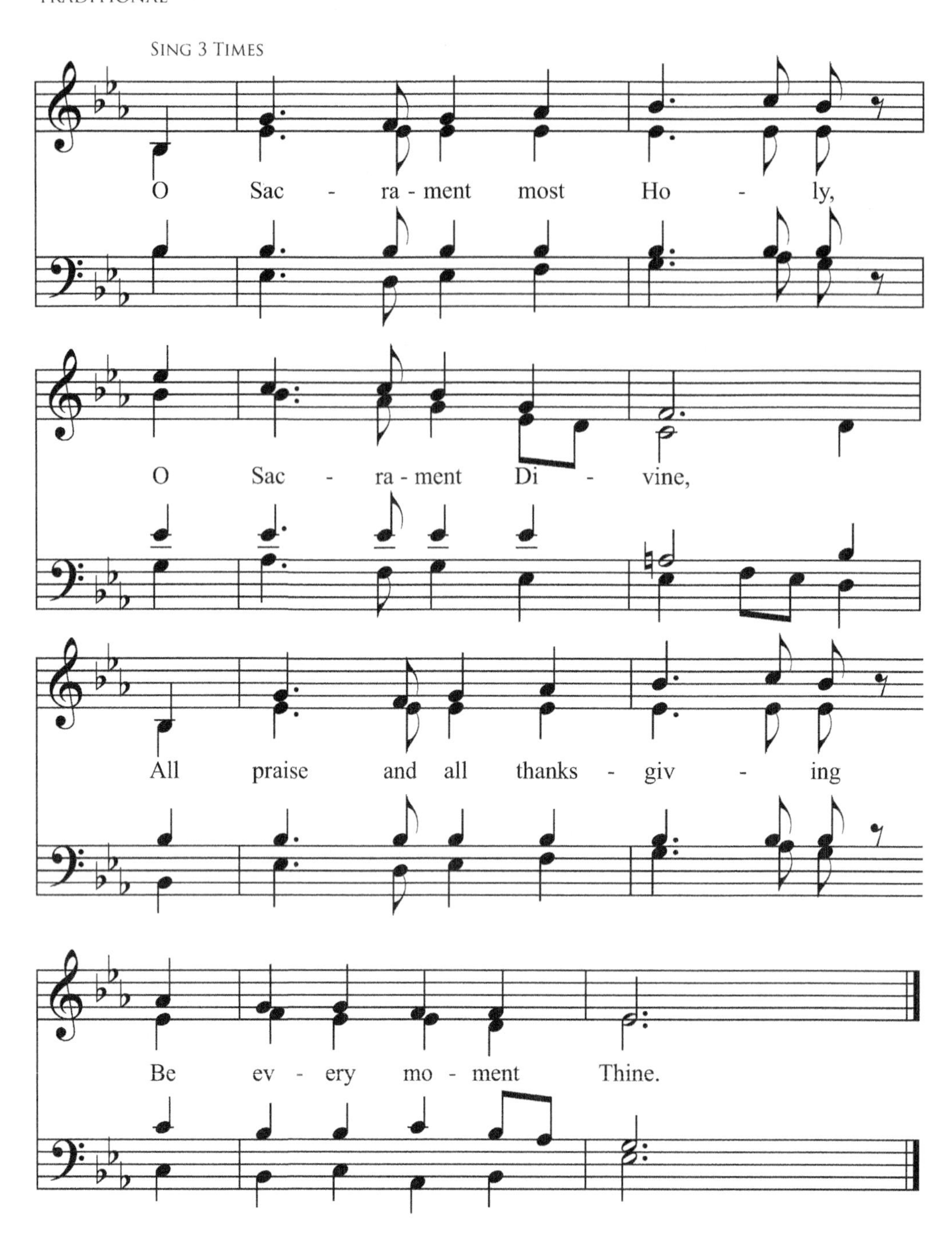

PANIS ANGELICUS

SACRIS SOLEMNIS 66. 66. 66. 8.   LOUIS LAMBILOTTE, S.J.

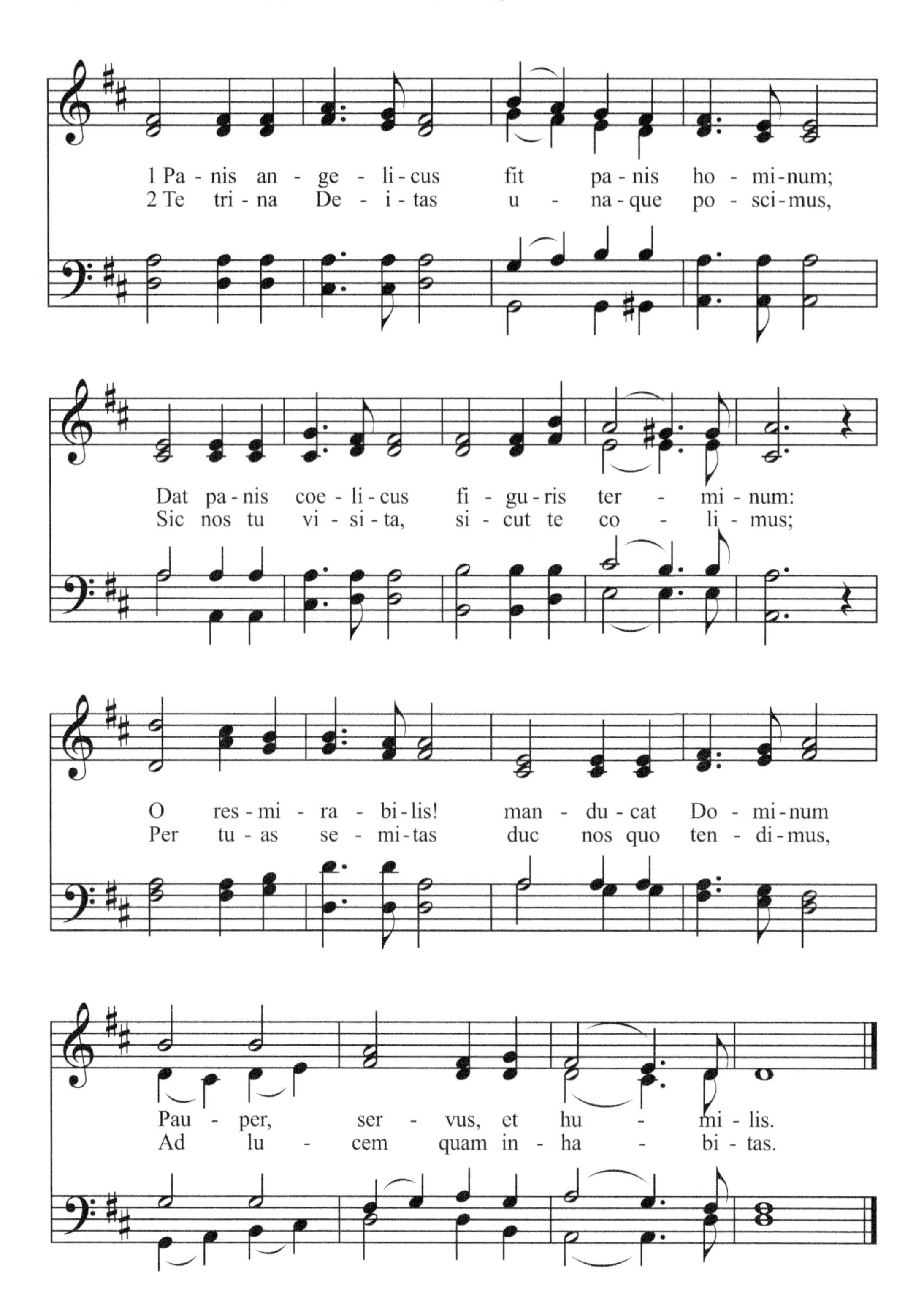

1 Pa - nis an - ge - li - cus fit pa - nis ho - mi - num;
2 Te tri - na De - i - tas u - na - que po - sci - mus,

Dat pa - nis coe - li - cus fi - gu - ris ter - mi - num:
Sic nos tu vi - si - ta, si - cut te co - li - mus;

O res mi - ra - bi - lis! man - du - cat Do - mi - num
Per tu - as se - mi - tas duc nos quo ten - di - mus,

Pau - per, ser - vus, et hu - mi - lis.
Ad lu - cem quam in - ha - bi - tas.

PEACE, PERFECT PEACE

SONG FORTY-SIX 10. 10. 10. 10. ORLANDO GIBBONS
EDWARD H. BICKERSTETH

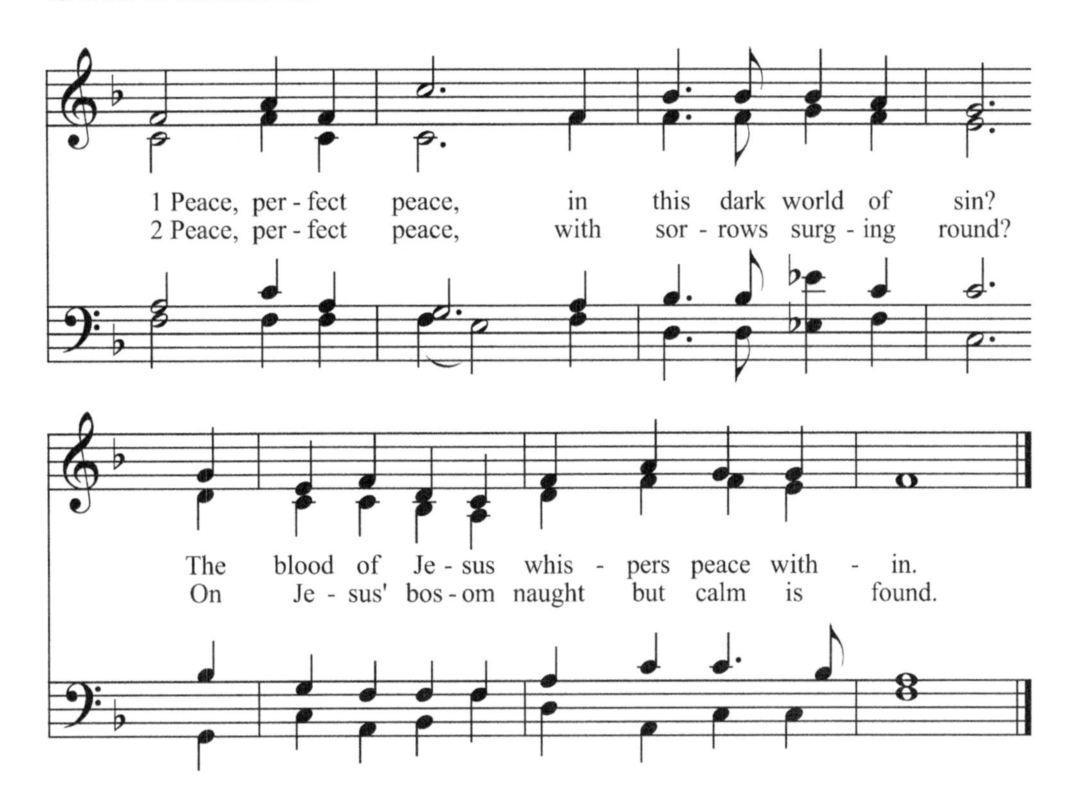

1 Peace, per-fect peace, in this dark world of sin?
2 Peace, per-fect peace, with sor-rows surg-ing round?

The blood of Je-sus whis-pers peace with-in.
On Jesus' bos-om naught but calm is found.

SOUL OF MY SAVIOR

ANIMA CHRISTI 10. 10. 10. 10.. WM. J. MAHER, S.J.
ANIMA CHRISTI

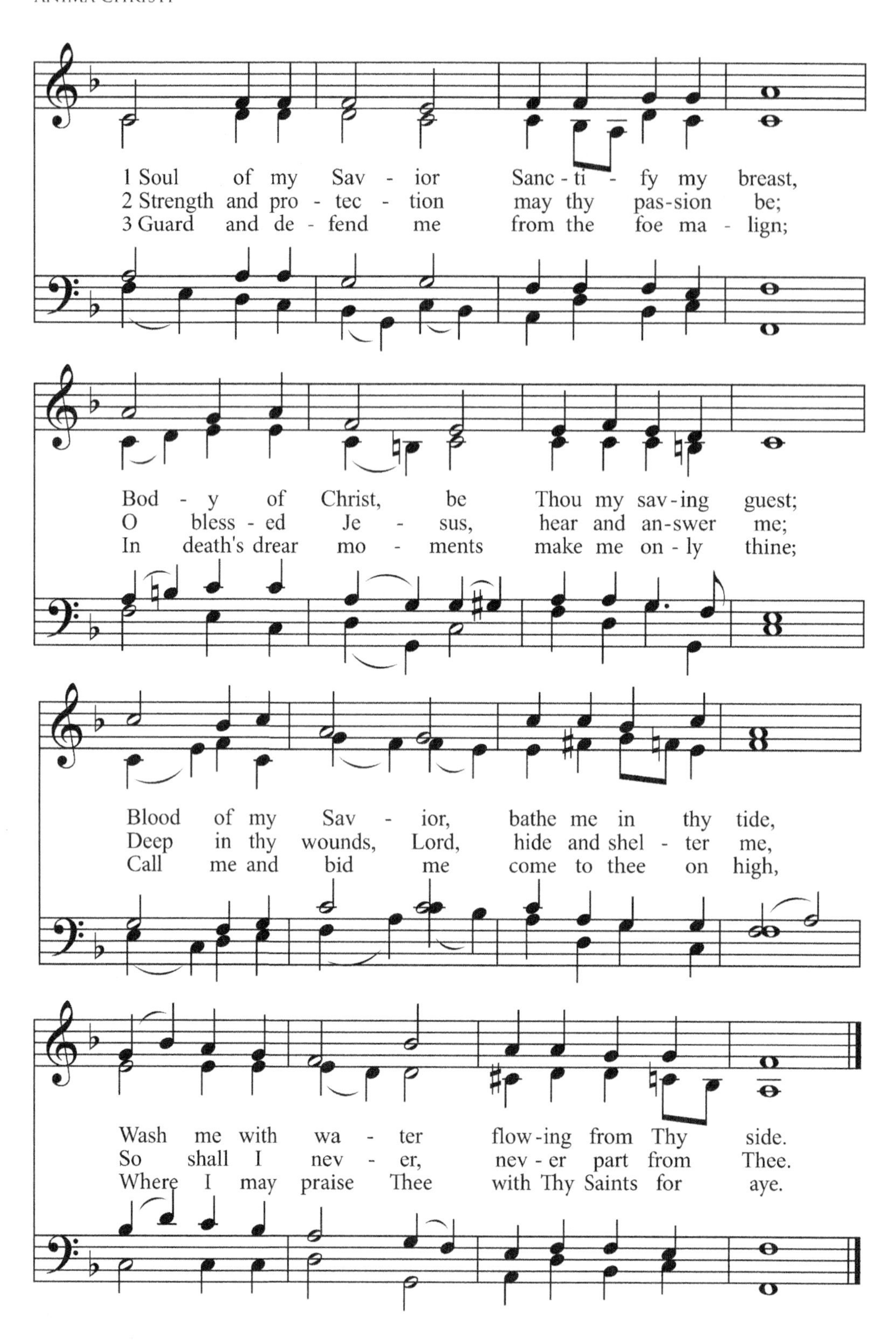

1 Soul of my Savior Sanc-ti-fy my breast,
2 Strength and pro-tec-tion may thy pas-sion be;
3 Guard and de-fend me from the foe ma-lign;

Bod-y of Christ, be Thou my sav-ing guest;
O bless-ed Je-sus, hear and an-swer me;
In death's drear mo-ments make me on-ly thine;

Blood of my Sav-ior, bathe me in thy tide,
Deep in thy wounds, Lord, hide and shel-ter me,
Call me and bid me come to thee on high,

Wash me with wa-ter flow-ing from Thy side.
So shall I nev-er, nev-er part from Thee.
Where I may praise Thee with Thy Saints for aye.

SOUL OF MY SAVIOR

GREENFIELD 10. 10. 10. 10.. ANDREW GREEN O.S.B.
ANIMA CHRISTI

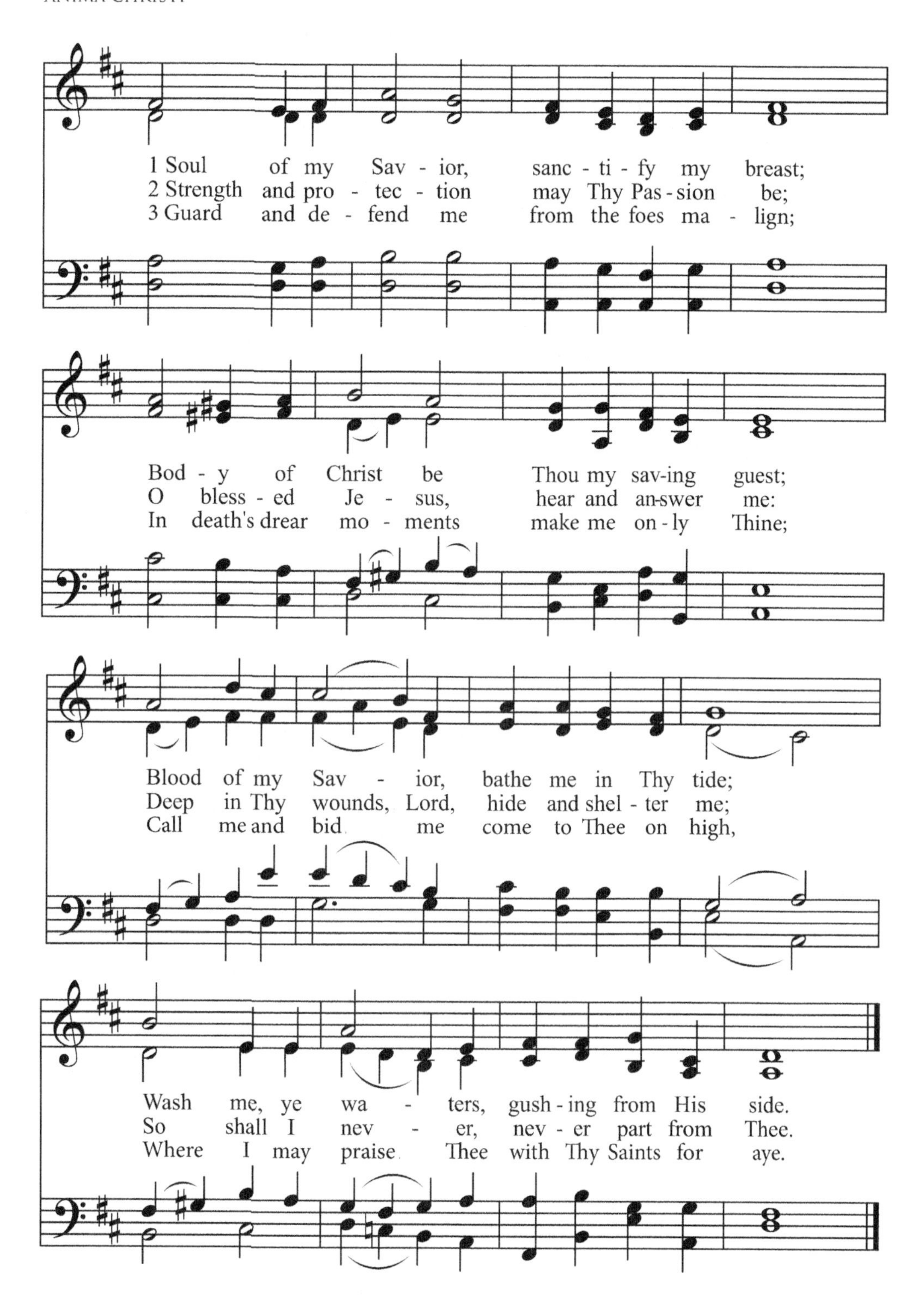

1 Soul of my Savior, sanctify my breast;
Body of Christ be Thou my saving guest;
Blood of my Savior, bathe me in Thy tide;
Wash me, ye waters, gushing from His side.

2 Strength and protection may Thy Passion be;
O blessed Jesus, hear and answer me:
Deep in Thy wounds, Lord, hide and shelter me;
So shall I never, never part from Thee.

3 Guard and defend me from the foes malign;
In death's drear moments make me only Thine;
Call me and bid me come to Thee on high,
Where I may praise Thee with Thy Saints for aye.

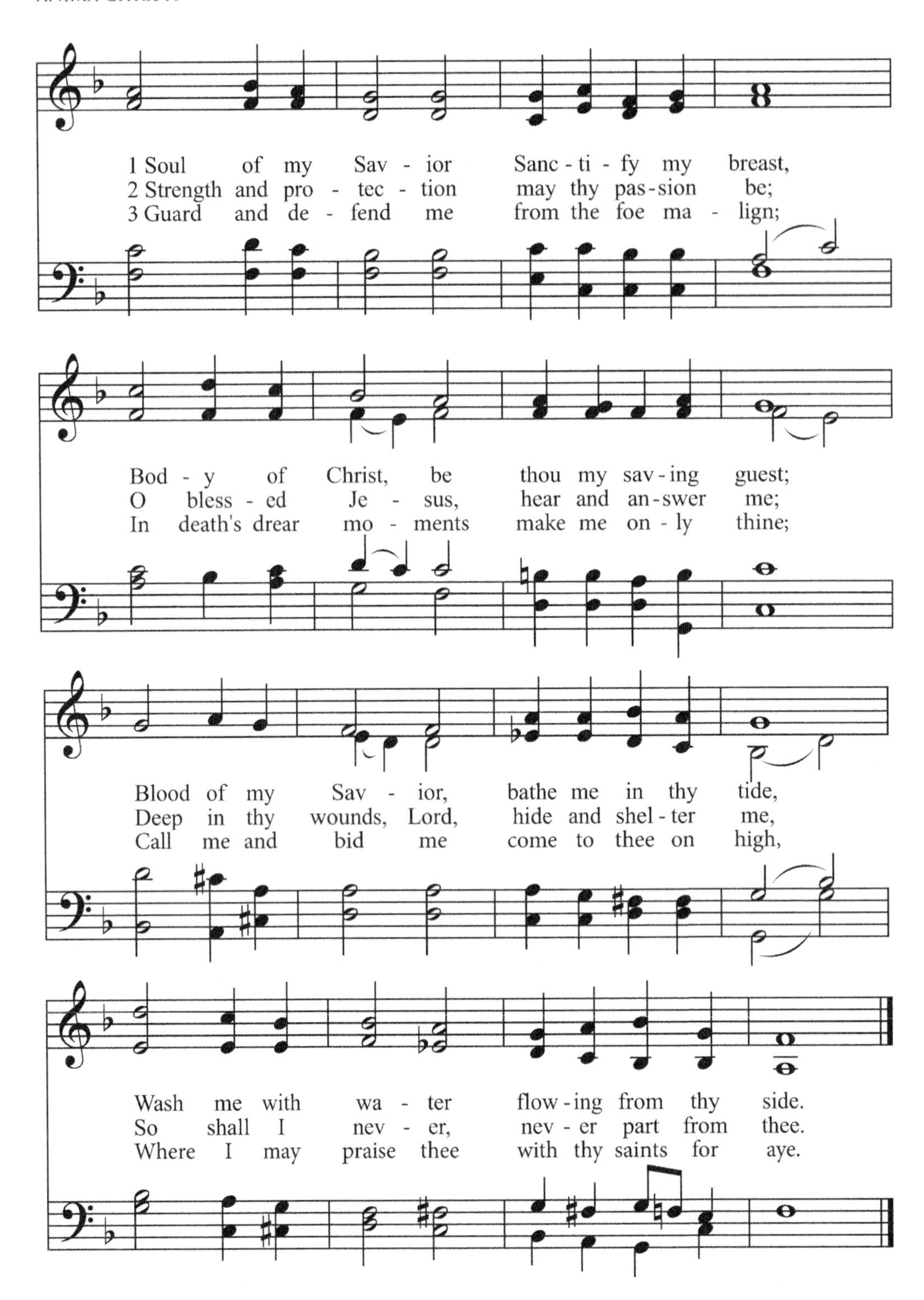

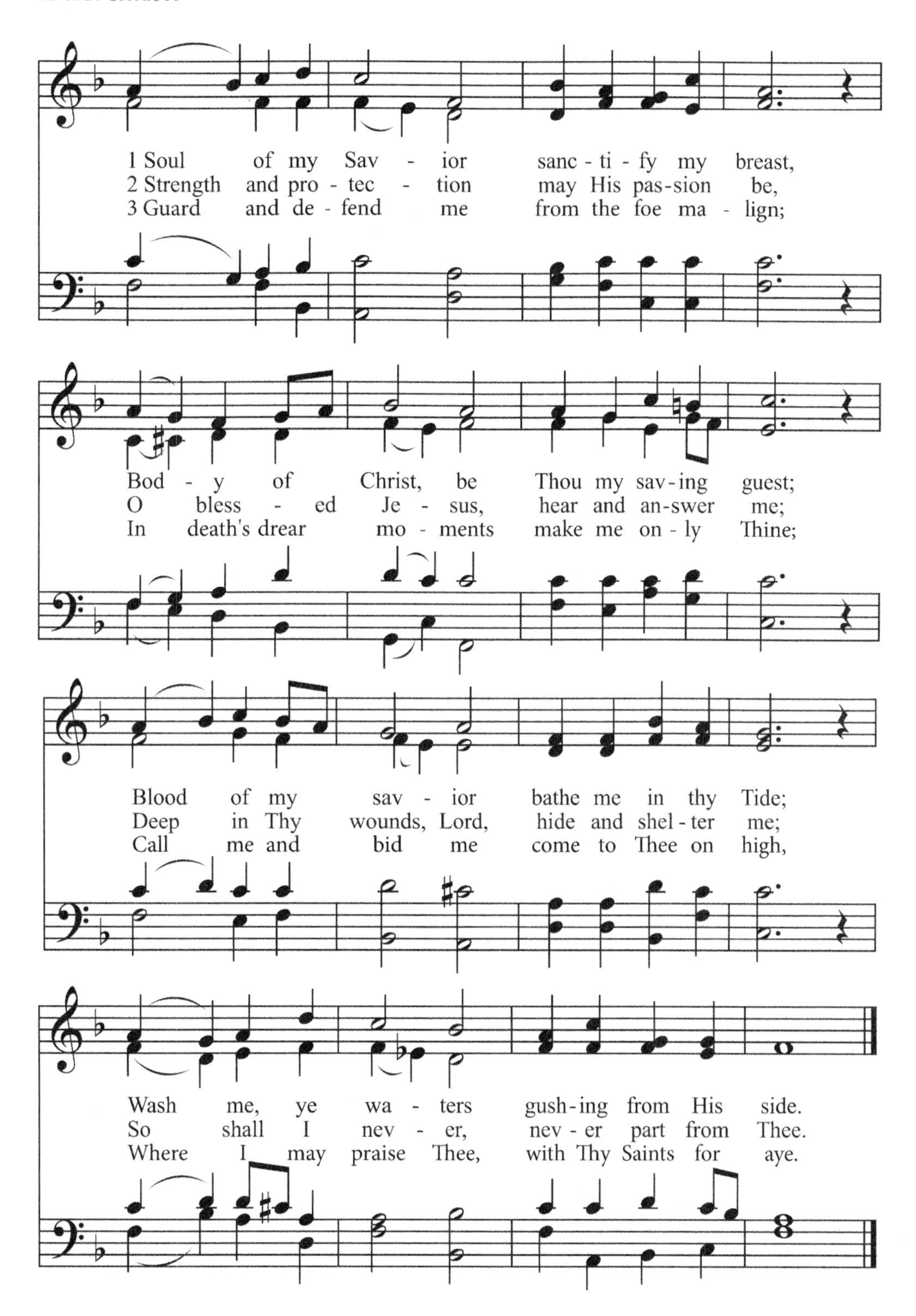

SOUL OF MY SAVIOUR

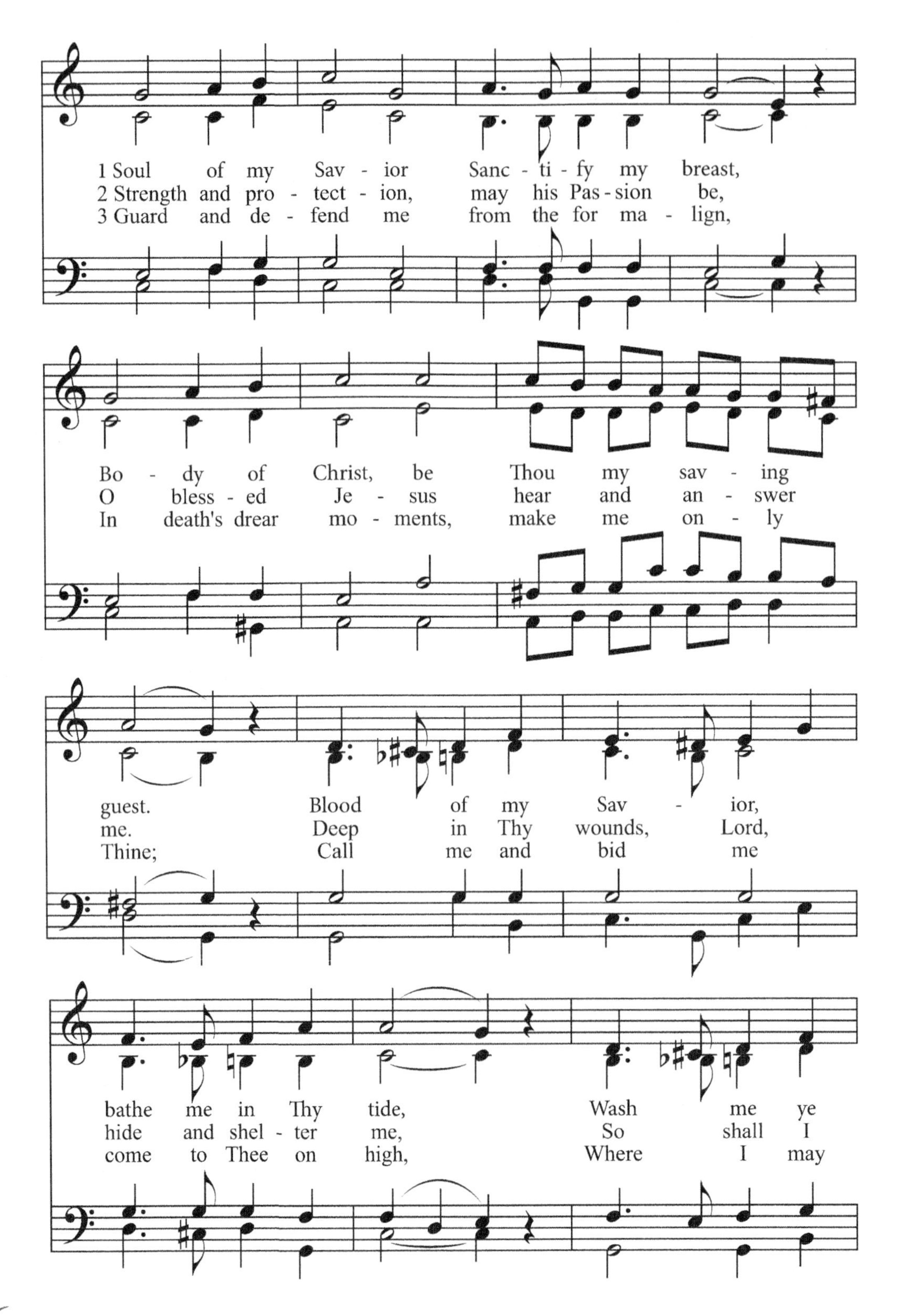

1 Soul of my Savior Sanc-ti-fy my breast, Bo-dy of Christ, be Thou my sav-ing guest. Blood of my Sav-ior, bathe me in Thy tide, Wash me ye
2 Strength and pro-tect-ion, may his Pas-sion be, O bless-ed Je-sus hear and an-swer me. Deep in Thy wounds, Lord, hide and shel-ter me, So shall I
3 Guard and de-fend me from the foe ma-lign, In death's drear mo-ments, make me on-ly Thine; Call me and bid me come to Thee on high, Where I may

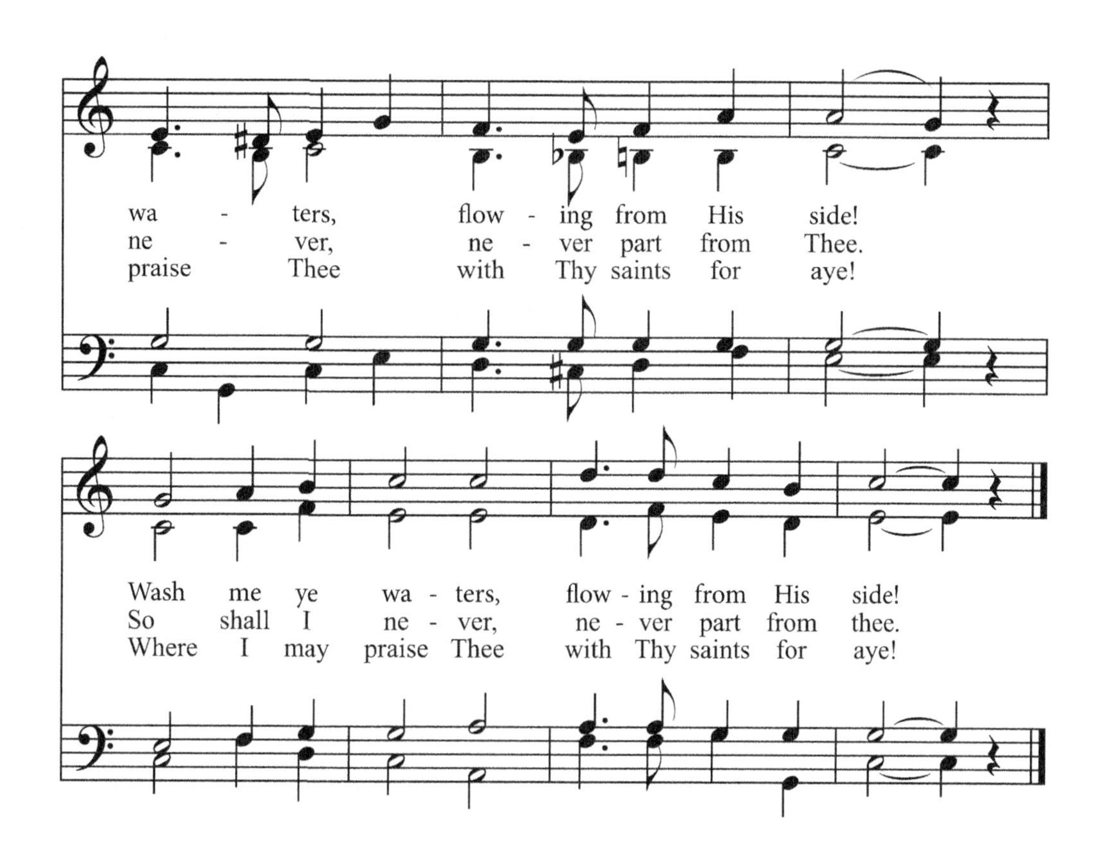

wa - ters, flow - ing from His side!
ne - ver, ne - ver part from Thee.
praise Thee with Thy saints for aye!
Wash me ye wa - ters, flow - ing from His side!
So shall I ne - ver, ne - ver part from thee.
Where I may praise Thee with Thy saints for aye!

SWEET SACRAMENT DIVINE!

STANFIELD 66. 66. 88. 66. FR. E. STANFIELD

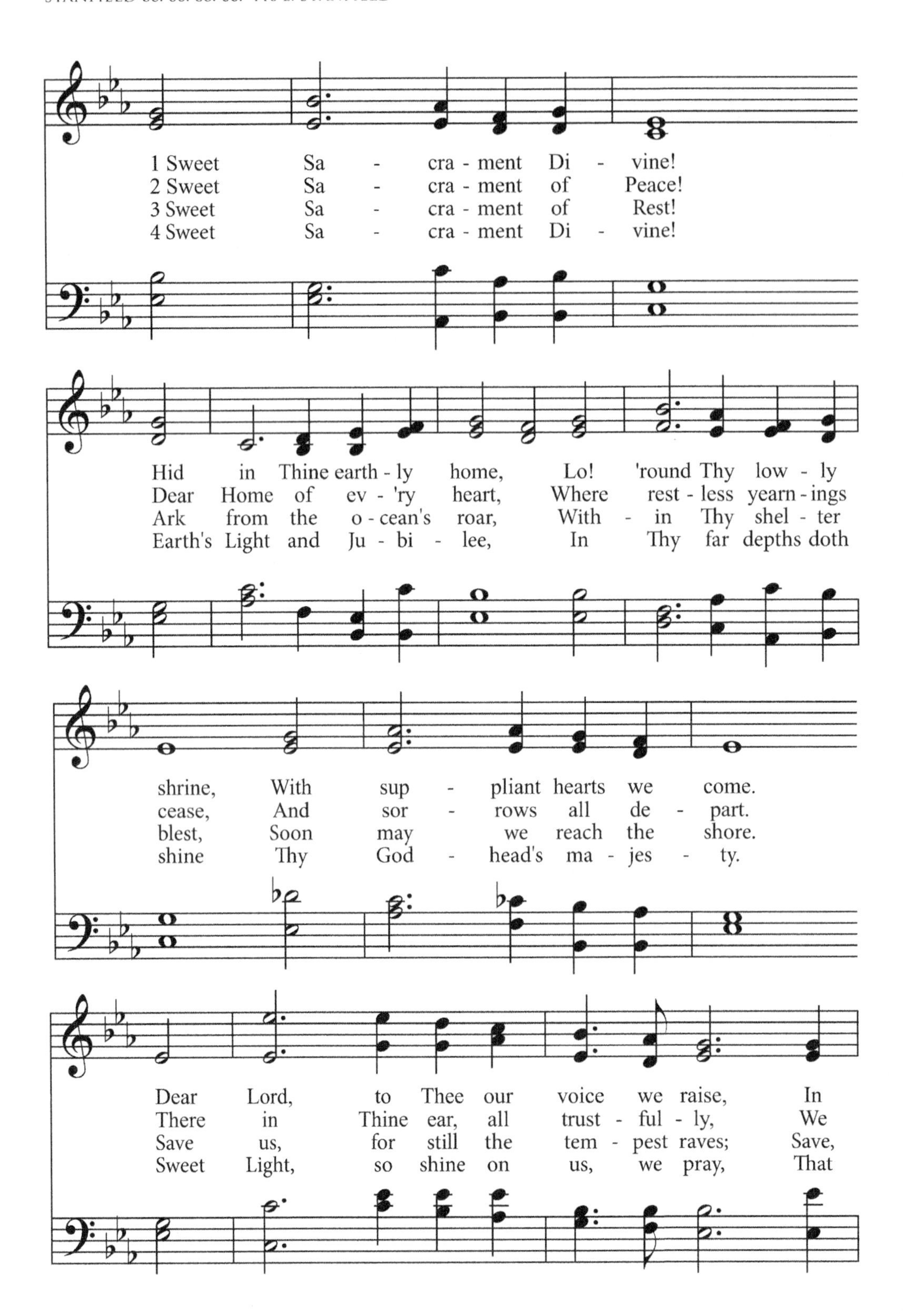

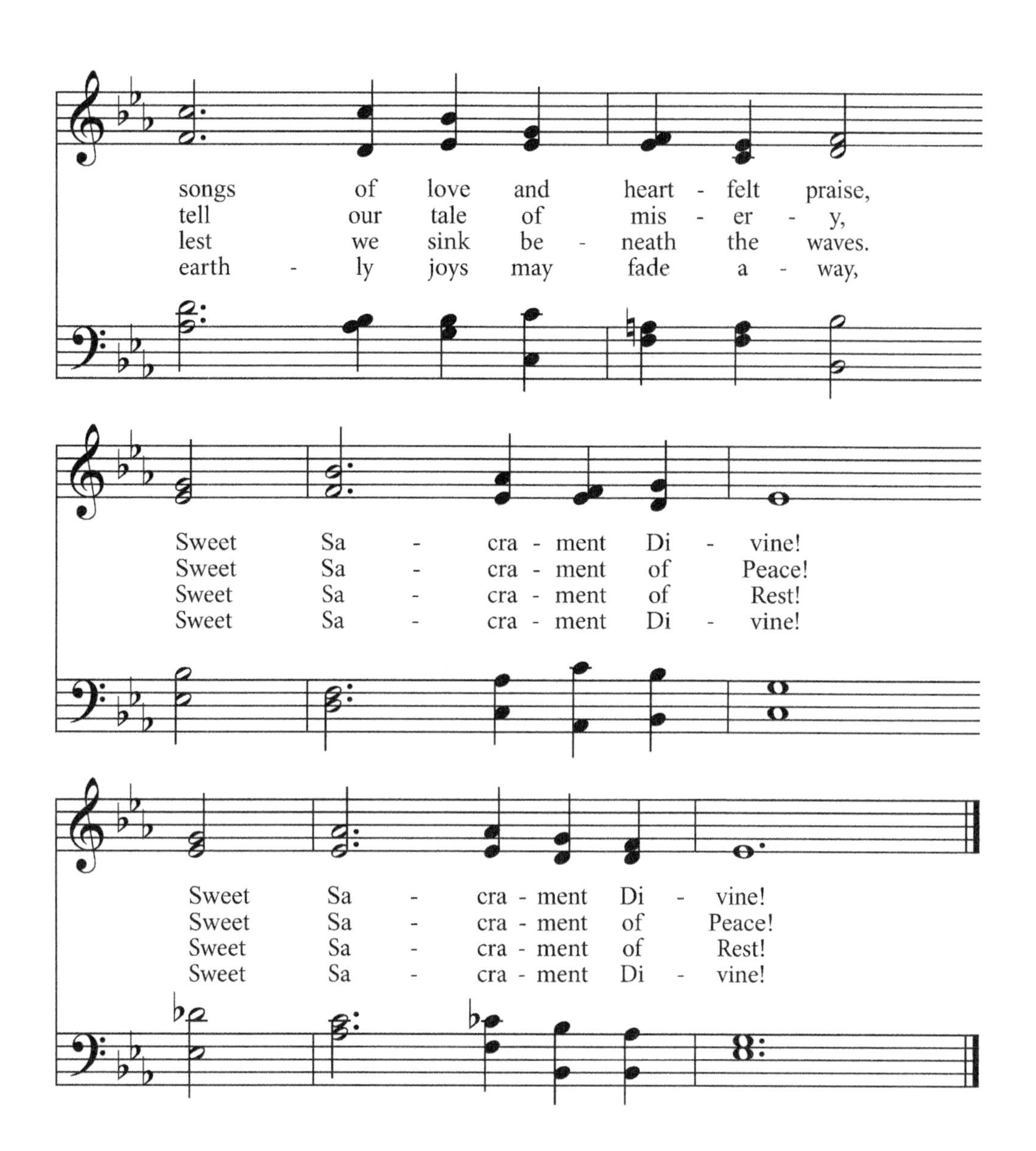
songs of love and heart - felt praise,
tell our tale of mis - er - y,
lest we sink be - neath the waves.
earth - ly joys may fade a - way,
Sweet Sa - cra - ment Di - vine!
Sweet Sa - cra - ment of Peace!
Sweet Sa - cra - ment of Rest!
Sweet Sa - cra - ment Di - vine!
Sweet Sa - cra - ment Di - vine!
Sweet Sa - cra - ment of Peace!
Sweet Sa - cra - ment of Rest!
Sweet Sa - cra - ment Di - vine!

THE KING OF HEAVEN

DUNDEE 87. 87. SCOTTISH PSALTER
PHILIP DODDRIDGE

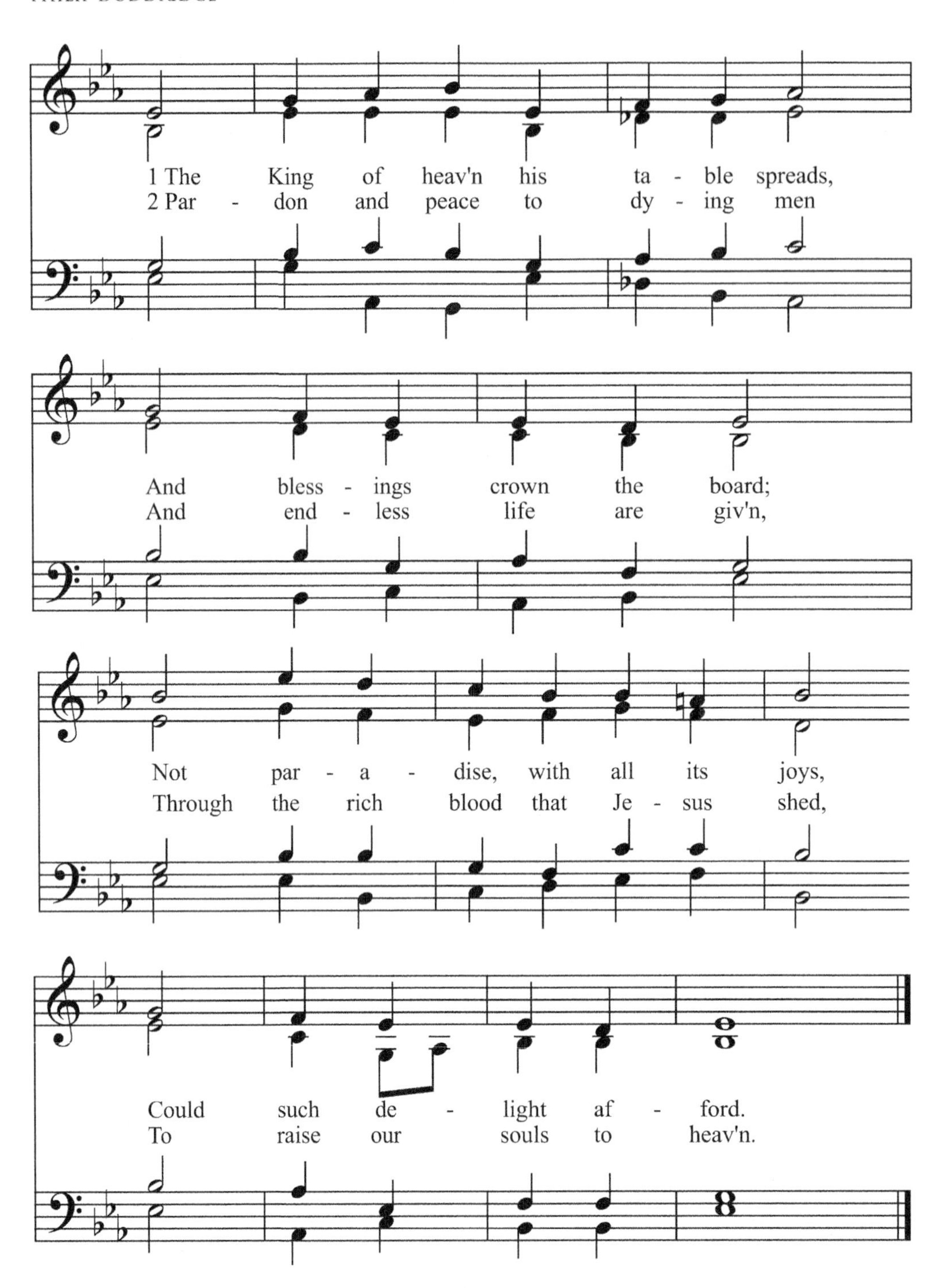

1 The King of heav'n his table spreads,
And blessings crown the board;
Not paradise, with all its joys,
Could such delight afford.

2 Pardon and peace to dying men
And endless life are giv'n,
Through the rich blood that Jesus shed,
To raise our souls to heav'n.

THE VERY ANGEL'S BREAD

CRISWELL 66. 56. 66. 8 P. MEURERS HARM. ©2009 MARK WINCHESTER
PANIS ANGELICUS

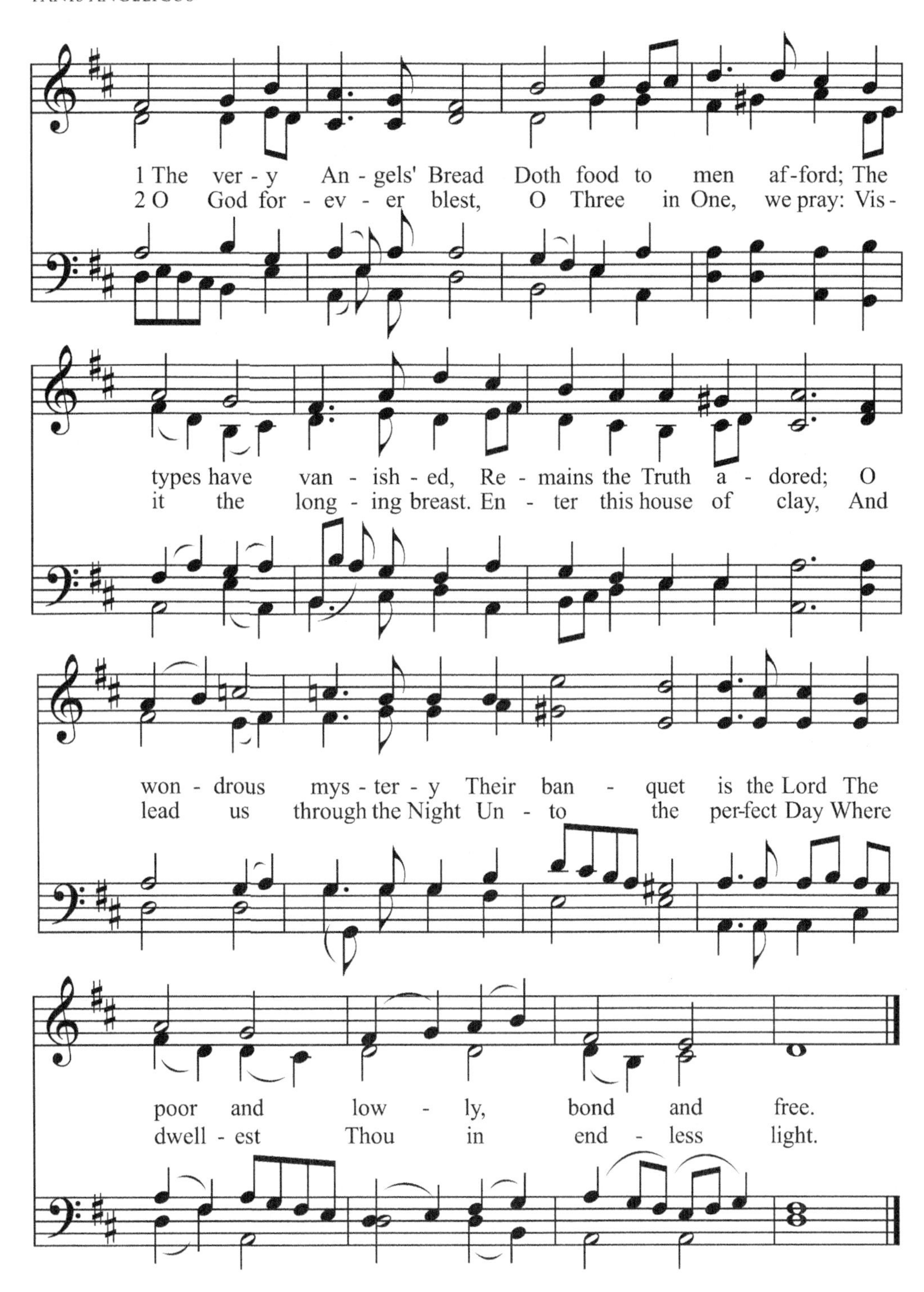

1 The very Angels' Bread Doth food to men afford; The types have vanished, Remains the Truth adored; O wondrous mystery Their banquet is the Lord The poor and lowly, bond and free.

2 O God forever blest, O Three in One, we pray: Visit the longing breast. Enter this house of clay, And lead us through the Night Unto the perfect Day Where dwellest Thou in endless light.

THIS IS THE HOUR

SONG TWENTY-TWO 10. 10. 10. 10. ORLANDO GIBBONS
HORATIUS BONAR

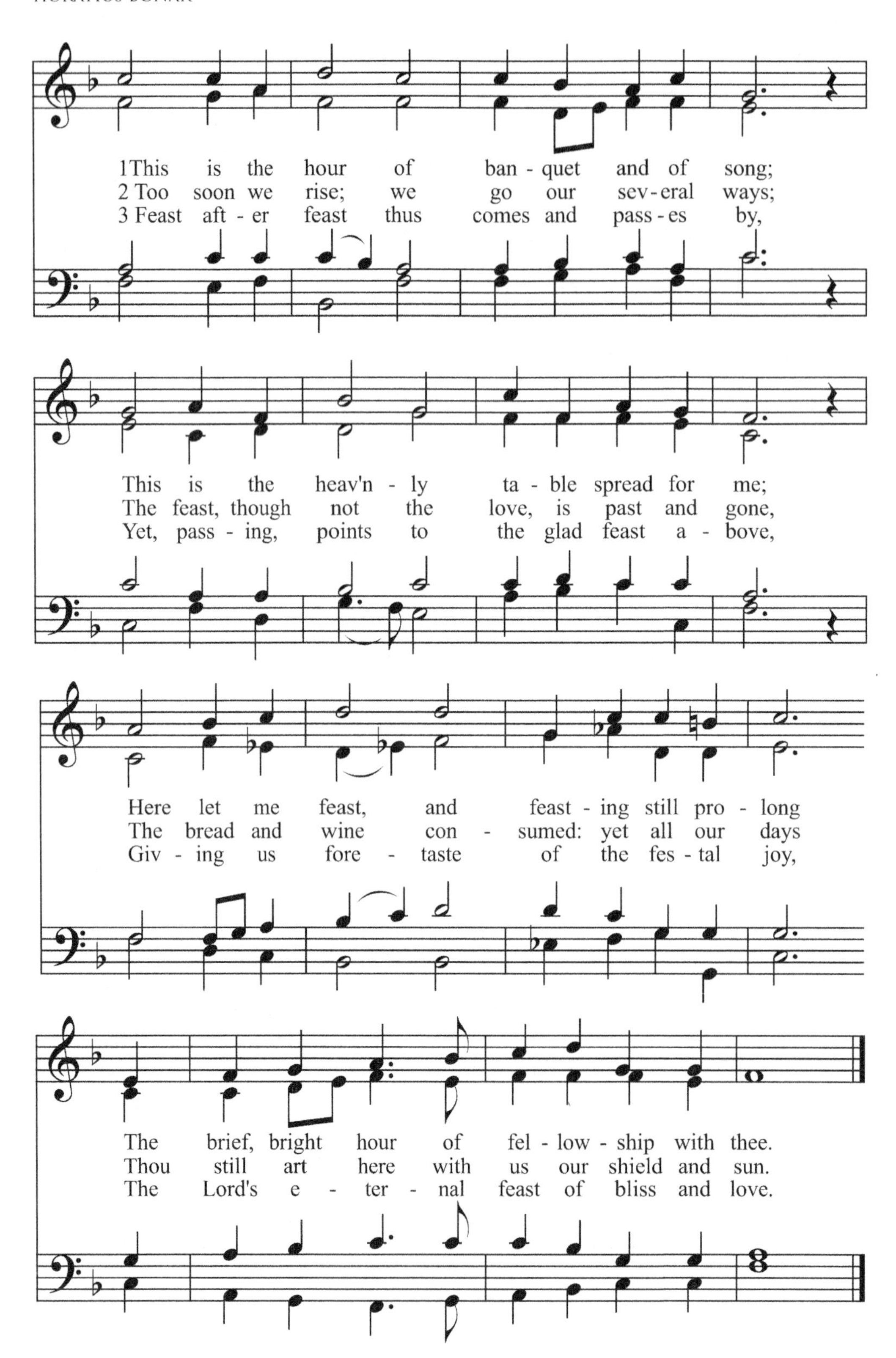

1. This is the hour of banquet and of song;
This is the heav'nly table spread for me;
Here let me feast, and feasting still prolong
The brief, bright hour of fellowship with thee.

2. Too soon we rise; we go our sev-eral ways;
The feast, though not the love, is past and gone,
The bread and wine consumed: yet all our days
Thou still art here with us our shield and sun.

3. Feast after feast thus comes and passes by,
Yet, passing, points to the glad feast above,
Giving us foretaste of the festal joy,
The Lord's eternal feast of bliss and love.

WE THEE ADORE

MANNE 10. 10. WITH REFRAIN JOSEPH MICHAEL HAYDN
ADORO TE

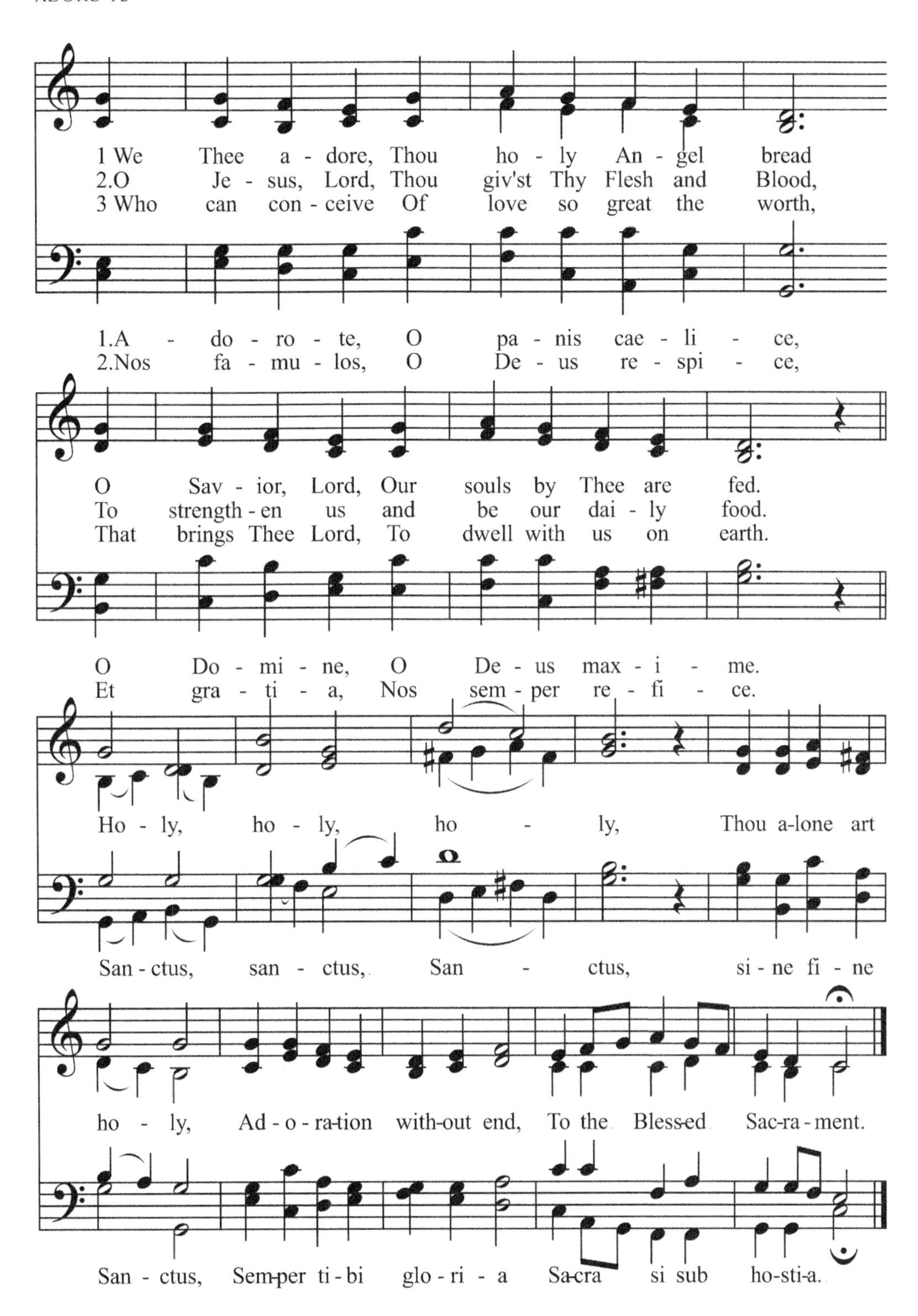

WHAT HAPPINESS CAN EQUAL MINE?

SWEET EMBRACE L.M.
REV. F.W. FABER

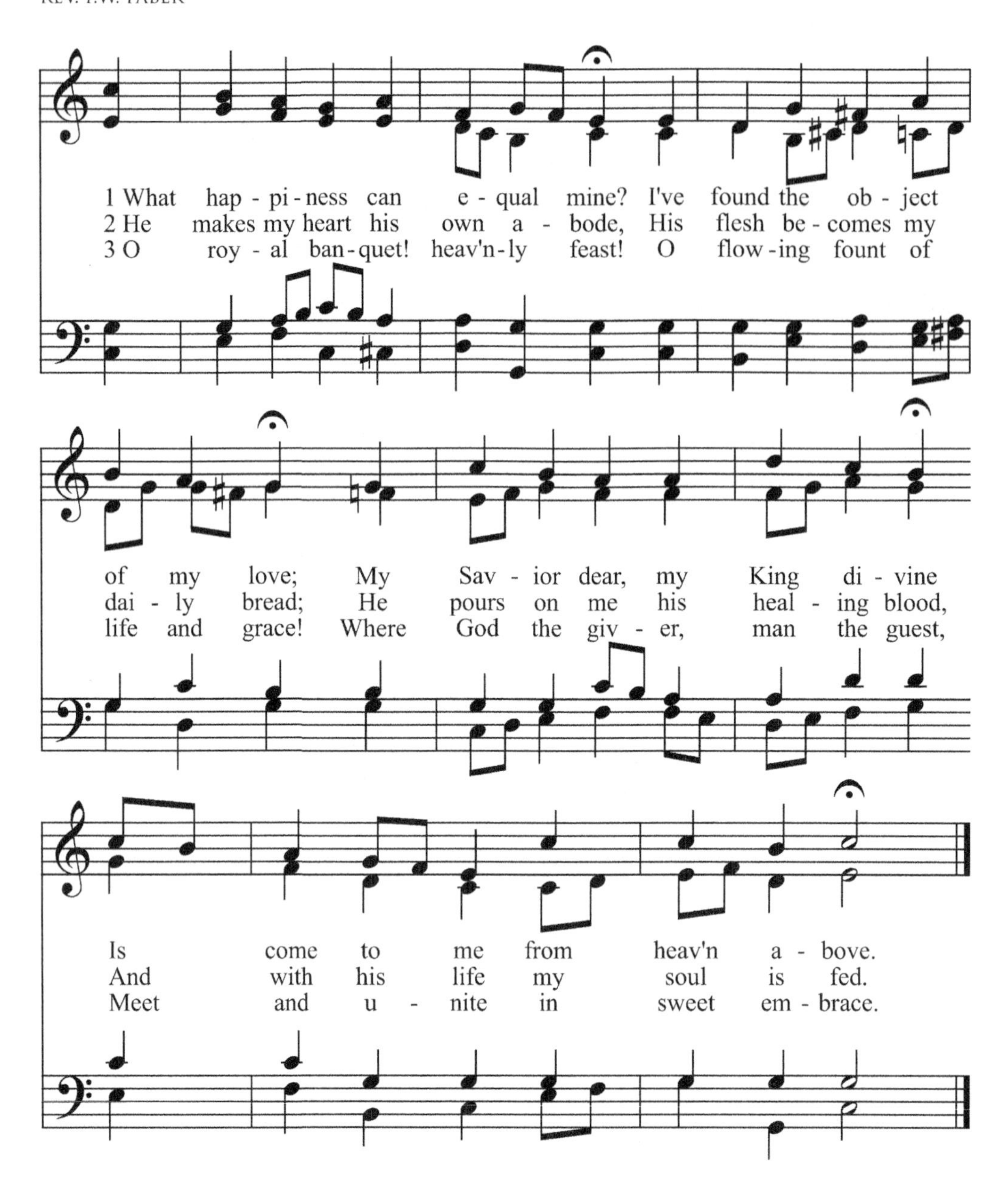

1. What happiness can equal mine? I've found the object of my love; My Savior dear, my King divine Is come to me from heav'n above.

2. He makes my heart his own abode, His flesh becomes my daily bread; He pours on me his healing blood, And with his life my soul is fed.

3. O royal banquet! heav'nly feast! O flowing fount of life and grace! Where God the giver, man the guest, Meet and unite in sweet embrace.

WHAT HAPPINESS CAN EQUAL MINE?

SACRED BANQUET L.M.
REV. F.W. FABER

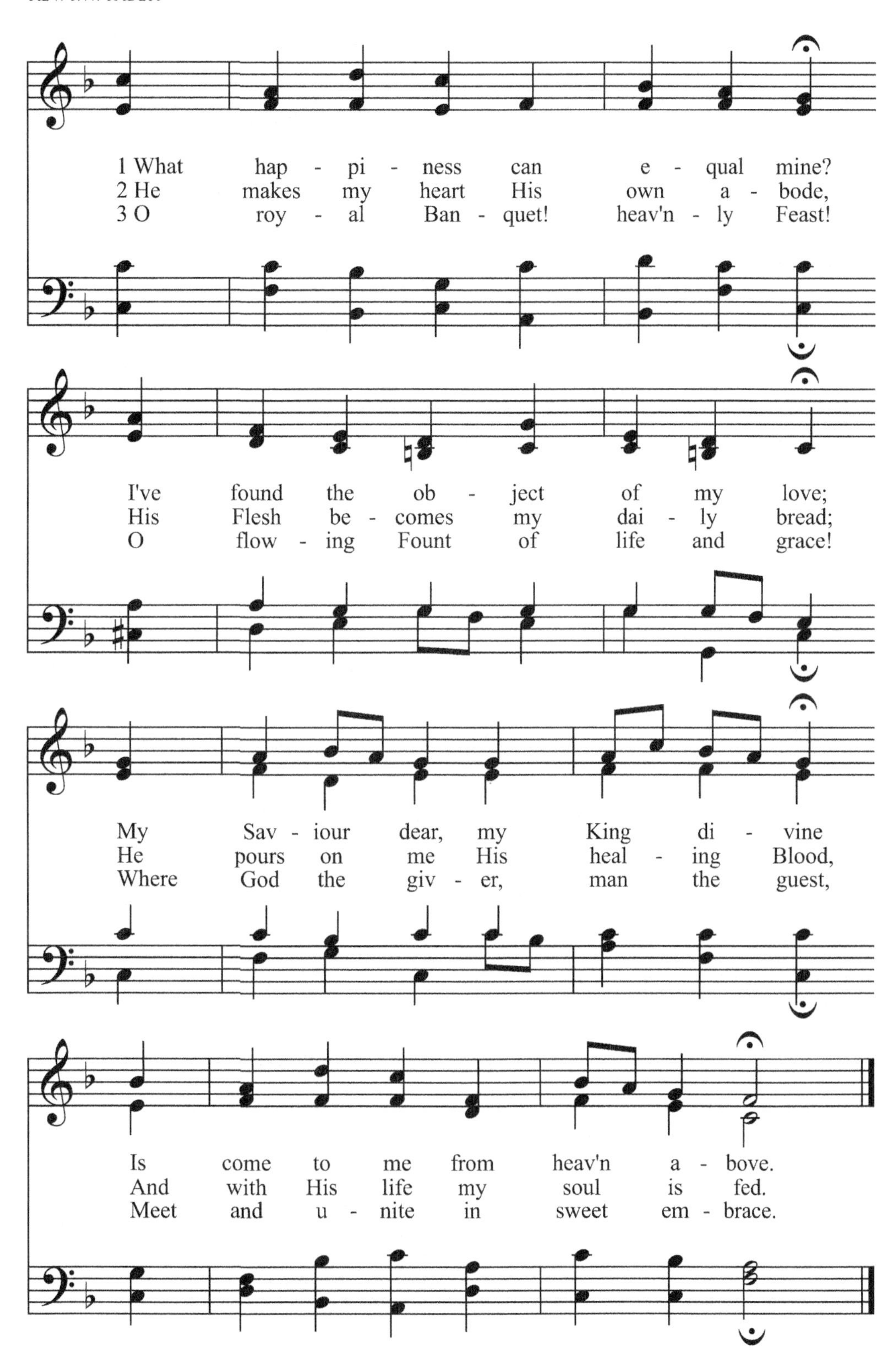

1 What happiness can equal mine?
I've found the object of my love;
My Saviour dear, my King divine
Is come to me from heav'n above.

2 He makes my heart His own abode,
His Flesh becomes my daily bread;
He pours on me His healing Blood,
And with His life my soul is fed.

3 O royal Banquet! heav'nly Feast!
O flowing Fount of life and grace!
Where God the giver, man the guest,
Meet and unite in sweet embrace.

WORD OF GOD

DRAKES BOUGHTON 87. 87. EDWARD ELGAR
CAMPBELL

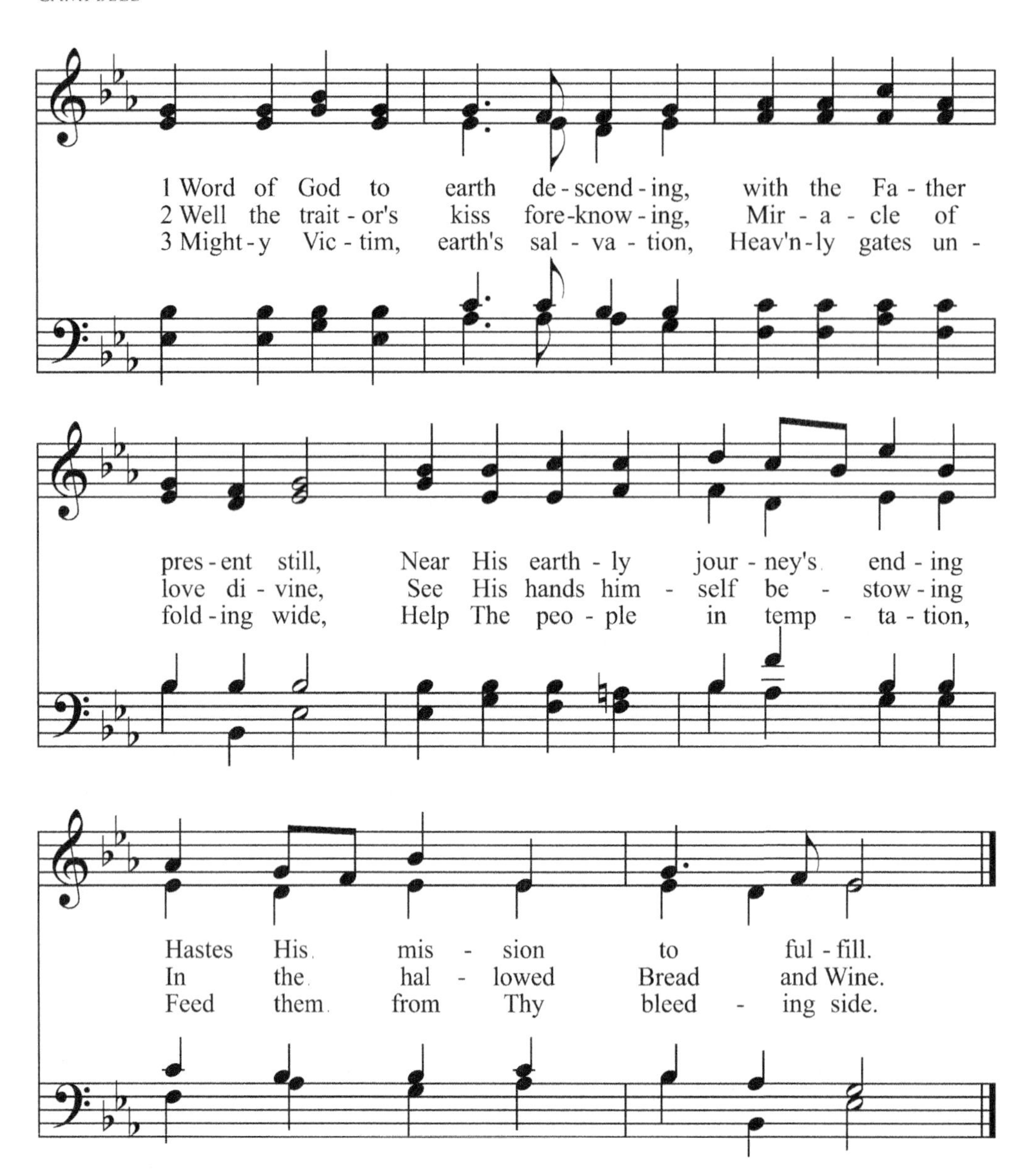

1 Word of God to earth descending, with the Father present still, Near His earthly journey's ending, Hastes His mission to fulfill.
2 Well the traitor's kiss foreknowing, Miracle of love divine, See His hands himself bestowing In the hallowed Bread and Wine.
3 Mighty Victim, earth's salvation, Heav'nly gates unfolding wide, Help The people in temptation, Feed them from Thy bleeding side.

INDEX OF HYMNS

According To Thy Gracious word 1
And I Shall See His Face 2
Be Known To Us In Breaking Bread 3
Be Known To Us In Breaking Bread 4
Deck Thyself, My Soul, With Gladness 6
Draw Nigh And Take The Body Of The Lord ... 8
Drop, Drop, Slow Tears 9
Hail! Thou Living Bread 10
Here, O My Lord, I See Thee Face To Face 11
Holy! Holy! Holy! Holy! 12
In This Sacrament, Sweet Jesus 13
In This Sacrament, Sweet Jesus 14
In This Sacrament, Sweet Jesus 16
Jesus, Food Of Angels 18
Jesus, Food Of Angels 19
Jesus, Gentlest Savior 20
Jesus, Gentlest Savior 22
Jesus, Jesus, Come To Me 24
Jesus, Jesus, Come To Me 26
Jesus, Lord, Be Thou My Own 28
Jesus, My Lord, My God, My All 30
Jesus, Thou Art Coming 32
Jesus, Thou Art Coming 33
Jesus, Thou Art Coming 34
Jesus, Thou Art Coming 35
My God, And Is Thy Table Spread 36
My God, Thy Table Now Is Spread 37
Now, My Tongue, The Mystery 38
O Bread Of Heav'n 40
O Bread Of Heav'n 42
O Christ, To You We Bring Our Weary Souls .. 44

O Christ, To You We Bring Our Weary Souls .. 46
O Food That Weary Pilgrims Love 48
O Food, The Pilgrim Needeth 50
O Food, The Pilgrim Needeth 51
O God, Unseen, Yet Ever Near 52
O Godhead Hid 54
O Jesus Christ, Redeemer 56
O Jesus Christ, Redeemer 58
O Jesus, Thou The Glory Art 60
O Jesus, Lord, Most Mighty king 61
O Jesus, Lord, Remember 62
O Lord, I Am Not Worthy 64
O Lord, I Am Not Worthy 66
O Lord, I Am Not Worthy 67
O Sacrament Most Holy 68
Panis Angelicus 70
Peace, Perfect Peace 71
Soul Of My Savior 72
Soul Of My Savior 73
Soul Of My Savior 74
Soul Of My Savior 75
Soul Of My Savior 76
Sweet Sacrament Divine! 78
The King Of Heav'n His Table Spreads 80
The Very Angels' Bread 81
This Is The Hour Of Banquet And Of Song 82
We Thee adore 83
What Happiness Can Equal Mine? 84
What Happiness Can Equal Mine? 85
Word Of God To Earth Descending 86

The creative commons photo of St Vitus Cathedral in the Czech Republic by David Iliff on the back cover is presented under the terms of http://creativecommons.org/licenses/by-sa/2.5/

Printed in Great Britain
by Amazon